9TH BIBLE READING MARATHON
A 26-Week Topical Bible Reading Schedule

Another Chapter from God's Book
- Memorable Chapters of the Bible

Gresham R. Holton, *Ph.D.*

Scripture Text Contributors
Homer Anderson
Myra Anderson
Kevin Boyd
Byron Brown
Janet Brown
Jerry Deloach
Marilyn King
John King
John Klimko
Ruth Harrison
Kenny Holton
G. R. Holton
John Hunt
Carrie Seat
Don Seat
Toni Webb
Ronnie West
Leon Weeks
Marie Weeks

◊ *Bible Reading Marathons are designed to encourage people to read the Bible.*

◊ *We believe regular reading of the Bible builds faith in God.*

◊ *We believe the Bible is the inerrant, inspired Word of God.*

◊ *We believe reading the Bible should be a regular habit for faithful Christians.*

◊ *We believe a Christian's life is faith in action.*

Sponsored and Supported by the
CENTRAL AVENUE CHURCH OF CHRIST - 304 EAST CENTRAL AVENUE - VALDOSTA, GEORGIA 31601
PHONE: (229) 242-6115 Website: www.cacoc.co

No. 9 in BIBLE READING MARATHON Series

Another Chapter from God's Book
A 26-Week Bible Reading Schedule
Memorable Chapters of the Bible

Gresham R. Holton, *Ph.D.*
CONTACT: grholton@yahoo.com

Copy Review Editor
Toni Ellen Webb

Background Cover Image
John Klimko

Growing Panes Articles
G. R. Holton

Published by
GROWING PANES, INC.
3543 Raintree Drive
Valdosta, Georgia 31601

9th BIBLE READING MARATHON
A 26-Week Topical Bible Reading Series

Another Chapter from God's Book
- Memorable Chapters from the Bible

Scripture Contributors	Reading Schedule
G. R. Holton	Week 1 **OUR GOD:** The Majesty of Almighty God
Myra Anderson	Week 2 **GLORY OF GOD:** The Incomparable Glory of Our God
Homer Anderson	Week 3 **GOD'S WORLD:** The Created, Spiritual and Worldly Universe
G. R. Holton	Week 4 **CONDEMNED BY SIN:** God Gave the World Up to Sin
Kevin Boyd	Week 5 **TRUE WORSHIP:** Acceptable Worship in Spirit and Truth
Byron Brown	Week 6 **VAIN & FALSE WORSHIP**: Unacceptable Worship and Idol Worship
Janet Brown	Week 7 **PRAISE AND PRAYER**: Bless the Lord, O My soul
Jerry Deloach	Week 8 **GIVING TO GOD**: Opening the Windows of Heaven
Ruth Harrison	Week 9 **GOD'S FAITHFULNESS:** Be Faithful
Kenny Holton	Week 10 **SERVANT-LEADERS FOR CHRIST**: Do as I have done, "Pick up your Towel."
John Hunt	Week 11 **DISBELIEF AND DISOBEDIENCE**: Ungodliness and disobedience
Marilyn King	Week 12 **PRACTICES OF RIGHTEOUSNESS:** Things that Pertain to Life and Godliness
John King	Week 13 **NEW BEGINNINGS:** Again! Starting Over.
John Klimko	Week 14 **SEEKING THE LOST:** Come Unto Me, I will Give You Rest
Carrie Seat	Week 15 **VICTORY IN JESUS:** Understanding the Greatness of God's Powers
Don Seat	Week 16 **GOD PROVIDES**: Search Me, O God, and Know My Heart
Toni Webb	Week 17 **GOD'S PROTECTION**: Be Strong in the Lord and the Power of His Might
Ronnie West	Week 18 **SACREDNESS OF MARRIAGE**: God Joins a Man and a Woman in Marriage
Leon Weeks	Week 19 **FREEDOM IN SERVING GOD**: In Matters of Faith and Opinions
Marie Weeks	Week 20 **SPIRITUAL FOOD**: Food that Satisfies Our Spiritual Desires
Myra Anderson	Week 21 **BEARING BURDENS FOR CHRIST**: Loads we Carry Fulfill the Law of Christ
Homer Anderson	Week 22 **FAITH AND OBEDIENCE**: We Must Faithfully Obey God
Byron Brown	Week 23 **WISDOM:** The Wisdom of God and the Wisdom of Men
Janet Brown	Week 24 **BLESSINGS**: Count Your Blessings, Name Them One by One
John Hunt	Week 25 **LOVE**: The Greatest of These is Love
G. R. Holton	Week 26 **THE END IN SIGHT:** Come Lord Jesus

Sponsored and Supported by the
Central Avenue Church of Christ
304 East Central Avenue - Valdosta, GA 31601
Www.cacoc.com

Another Chapter from God's Book
- Memorable Chapters of the Bible

God's Book

The Bible is the inspired, "God breathed" Word from God! God's Book is divided into 1,189 chapters, or literary divisions. The Book was written over a period of nearly 3000 years with 40 writers in two languages (Hebrew and koine Greek). There are more than 500 English translations of the Book.

This Book is a "lamp unto our feet and a light unto our path" as we go through life (Psalm 119:105). These Words encourage us when we walk the "valley of the shadow of death" (Psalm 23:4) and when our enemies attack (Psalm 22). This Book is the Sword of the Spirit from the mouth of Jesus (Revelation 1) to convict us of sin, correct our false beliefs and practices, and trains us for righteous living. God's Book was written by **"men (who) spoke from God as they were carried along by the Holy Spirit"** (2 Peter 1:21).

"For the word of God is alive and powerful. It is sharper than the sharpest two-edged sword, cutting between soul and spirit, between joint and marrow. It exposes our innermost thoughts and desires" (Hebrews 4:12 NLT).

This Book is *"Inspired by God and is useful to teach us what is true and to make us realize what is wrong in our lives. It corrects us when we are wrong and teaches us to do what is right. God uses it to prepare and equip his people to do every good work"* (2 Timothy 2:16-17 NLT).

Memorable Chapters of the Bible

Every Bible student has a favorite chapter. That chapter may be 1 Corinthians 13 where the powerful force of love is outlined, or 1 John 4 where God's love is praised. Another student would pick Romans 8 which reveals that nothing can separate us from the Love of God. According to numerous surveys, more people choose the short Psalms 23 chapter as their favorite.

The 9th Bible Reading Marathon is a compilation of twenty-six (26) chapters of the Bible arbitrarily selected as "memorable." These are listed in the *Fast Track* readings. In most cases the *Fast Track* scriptures center around a topic selected from the readings. The *Middle Lane* includes readings that comment or cross-reference the chapters in the *Fast Track.* From the *Inside Track* each BRM runner can commit to memory key verses from the other readings. Experienced runners may read all three tracks, while others may choose to read either or both the *Middle Lane* and the *Inside Track.*

The important thing is for you to get into the race! Make Bible reading a regular habit.

Psalm 119

The Longest Chapter in the Bible

The longest chapter in God's Book is the longest Psalm with 176 contiguous verses. It is a Psalm of praise for the Word of God. This Psalm praises the *wonders* of God's Book, the Bible. Perhaps Psalm 119 is placed at the very middle of God's Book to red line the reasons why we need to read it daily.

Each day we face issues, troubles, challenges, and opportunities that we might not recognize much less even know how to face them.

Reading God's Book teaches us lessons on spiritual survival. Psalm 119 is outlined by each stanza beginning with a letter of the Hebrew alphabet:

א
ALEPH
Vss 1-8 Important to honor and respect God's Word in daily living

ב
BETH
Vss 9-16 God's Word cleanses our path and purpose in life

ג
GIMEL
Vss 17-24 God's Word reveals wonderous things about God, self, and sin

ד
DALETH
Vss 25-32 The Bible strengthens us inwardly to be faithful

ה
HE
Vss 33-40 Living by His Word means commitment, joy, and confirmation

ו
WAW
Vss 41-48 God's Word gives us Answers, Liberty, and Confidence

ז
ZAYIN
Vss 49-56 The Word of God provides comfort and hope

ח
HETH

Vss 57-64 Keep God's commandments for God is gracious and loving, man is sinful

ט
TETH
Vss 65-72 The Word teaches us that God is good, and that afflictions refine us

י
YODH
Vss 73-80 God's Word will help manage our life relationships

כ
KAPH
Vss 81-88 God's Word helps us see that God hears, sees, and provides for us

ל
LAMEDH
Vss 89-96 His Word assures us that God is faithful and will save his people

מ
MEM
Vss 97-104 We love God's Word because it makes us upright and understanding

נ
NUN
Vss 105-112 God's Word is our Guide for our lives

ס
SAMEKH
Vss 113-120 We love the Word for it shields us from many things

ע
AYIN
Vss 121-128 God ensures our salvation if we love His commandments

פ

PE

Vss 129-136 His Word directs us regarding our soul, the problem of sin and our attitude

צ

TZADE

Vss 137-144 God's Word is righteous because God is righteous

ק

KOPH

Vss 145-152 The Book defines our personal relationship with God

ר

RESH

Vss 153-160 The Word of God is Truth and righteous judgments

ש

SIN AND SHIN

Vss 161-168 Loving God's Word brings blessings

ת

TAW

Vss 169-176 God's Word results in the submission of our self to God

Psalm 117

The Shortest Chapter in the Bible

The shortest chapter is only two verses, approximately thirty words, is the very middle chapter of God's Book. *But it is power-packed*! There are 594 chapters before it and 594 chapters after it.

Psalm 117 begins and ends with *Praise the Lord.* The shortest chapter captures the emotions we experience when we read God's Book! They are worth repeating! *Praise the Lord!*

Welcome!

With these words, the shortest chapter in God's Book, we welcome you to the *9ᵗʰ Bible Reading Marathon*. May God bless you as you read through some of the

Memorable Chapters of the Bible:

"PRAISE THE LORD, ALL YOU NATIONS.

PRAISE HIM, ALL YOU PEOPLE OF THE EARTH.

FOR HIS UNFAILING LOVE FOR US IS POWERFUL.

THE LORD'S FAITHFULNESS ENDURES FOREVER.

PRAISE THE LORD!" - **Psalm 117 NLT**

How sweet your words taste to me;
  they are sweeter than honey.
Your commandments give me understanding;
  no wonder I hate every false way of life.

Your word is a lamp to guide my feet
  and a light for my path.
I've promised it once, and I'll promise it again:
  I will obey your righteous regulations.
                    - Psalm 119: 103-106 NLT

Growing Panes

Another Chapter from God's Book   9th BIBLE READING MARATHON

**Let the word of Christ dwell in you richly in all wisdom,
teaching and admonishing one another
in psalms and hymns and spiritual songs,
singing with grace in your hearts to the Lord.
And whatever you do in word or deed,
do all in the name of the Lord Jesus,
giving thanks to God the Father through Him.**
- Colossians 3:16-17

As Christians, we let the ***Word of God*** richly take up residence in us through singing the hymns we love. Hymns are beloved because they share the richness of the gospel and the beauty of Jesus Christ in a memorable way. Thousands of angels sang in chorus at the birth of Jesus (Luke 2) and around the throne of God when we enter eternity (Revelation 4-5).

Hymns and other spiritual songs minister to our hearts, giving us hope and faith. They teach us to minister to each other. Hymns unite us as Christians and take our thoughts off ourselves and put them on Jesus.

Favorite older hymns that are in the Public Domain are placed throughout the 26-week readings to give us opportunities to pause and praise God in our Bible Reading Marathon race. Such will refresh our spirits like a cup of cold water to a runner.

*The Website https://Hymnary.org. was used extensively in building the pages of memorable hymns and the comments about the Hymns. **Hymnary.org**: A comprehensive index of over 1 million **hymn** texts, **hymn** tunes, and hymnals, with information on authors and composers, **lyrics** and scores of many **hymns**, and various media files. **Hymnary.org** also incorporates the Dictionary of North American Hymnology, an extensive collection of hymnals published before 1978. Hymnary.org is an online database of hymns, hymnodists and hymnals hosted by Calvin College's Calvin Institute of Christian Worship and Christian Classics Ethereal Library.

All hymns used in this publication are in the Public Domain and free of copyright restrictions.

All Hail the Power of Jesus' Name

1780

By Edward Perronet, 1721-1792

All hail the power of Jesus' name!
Let angels prostrate fall.
Bring forth the royal diadem,
and crown him Lord of all.
Bring forth the royal diadem,
and crown him Lord of all!

O chosen seed of Israel's race
now ransomed from the fall,
hail him who saves you by his grace,
and crown him Lord of all.
Hail him who saves you by his grace,
and crown him Lord of all!

Let every tongue and every tribe
responsive to his call,
to him all majesty ascribe,
and crown him Lord of all.
To him all majesty ascribe,
and crown him Lord of all!

Oh, that with all the sacred throng
we at his feet may fall!
We'll join the everlasting song
and crown him Lord of all.
We'll join the everlasting song
and crown him Lord of all.

This hymn is a declaration of praise, but it's also much more than that. The words both declare the majesty of Christ and give us the task of making that majesty known to all.

Like many hymns describing the glory of God and the hope that one day all people will see that glory, this hymn alludes to Philippians 2:9-11: "at the name of Jesus every knee should bow, in heaven and on earth and under the earth, and every tongue acknowledge that Jesus Christ is Lord, to the glory of God the Father."

We long for this day, and declare our hope in its arrival in the text of this hymn. But are we willing to declare that hope to those who have not heard it? The phrase, "Easier said than done" comes to mind here.

After we have sung these words of victory and longing, what do we do? Do we act on those words and turn our expectancy into realities? Or do we wait for someone else to do it for us?

The fourth stanza of this great hymn declares, "We'll join the everlasting song..." Everlasting means that we are a part of that song right now – as we lift our voices together.

Our God

1ST WEEK

Theme: *The Majesty of Almighty God*

INSIDE TRACK MEMORY VERSES	MIDDLE LANE SUPPORTING PASSAGES	FAST TRACK TOPICAL CHAPTERS
MONDAY - *Believe Me that I am in the Father and the Father in Me, or else believe Me for the sake of the works themselves.* John 14:11 NKJV	**MONDAY** Genesis 1: 1-2 Hebrews 11: 1-3 1 John 1: 1-4	**MONDAY** John 1
TUESDAY *For my thoughts are not your thoughts, neither are your ways my ways, declares the Lord.* Isaiah 55:8 ESV	**TUESDAY** Psalm 103 2 Samuel 7: 18-29 Isaiah 14: 24-27	**TUESDAY** Isaiah 55
WEDNESDAY *God, who made the world and everything in it, since He is Lord of heaven and earth, does not dwell in temples made with hands.* Acts 17:24 NKJV	**WEDNESDAY** Matthew 11: 25-26 Acts 14: 8-18 Romans 1: 21-24	**WEDNESDAY** Acts 17
THURSDAY *You are My flock, the sheep of My pasture, My people, and I am your God, declares the Lord GOD.* Ezekiel 34: 31 BSB	**THURSDAY** Ezekiel 34: 11-31 Romans 11: 11-24 1 Peter 2:9-12,25	**THURSDAY** John 10
FRIDAY *Now to Him who is able to do exceedingly abundantly above all that we ask or think, according to the power that works in us, to Him be glory in the church by Christ Jesus to all generations, forever and ever. Amen.* Ephesians 3:20-21 NKJV	**FRIDAY** 2 Peter 3: 18 Ephesians 4: 1-9 Psalm 133: 1-3	**FRIDAY** Ephesians 3

QUESTION:
Is God Worthy of Our Worship?

ANSWER: Volumes would be needed to adequately answer this question. Consider just three reasons we worship Him:

Our God is the one and only good God. The "goodness" of God was claimed by Jesus twice in the New Testament. The rich young ruler was told "God alone is good…"(Luke 18:18). Jesus also said, "I am the *good* shepherd" (John 10:11). In contrast, idols were vindictive, ugly, and mean to their worshippers. He cares for us.

Our God is always present. Wherever we can go and where we cannot go, God is there to accept our service.

"Where can I go from your Spirit? Where can I flee from your presence? If I go up to the heavens, you are there; if I make my bed in the depths, you are there. If I rise on the wings of the dawn, if I settle on the far side of the sea, even there your hand will guide me, your right hand will hold me fast" (Psalm 139:7–10 NIV).

Our God is all powerful. He always has all power over all things and in all ways. God's power is demonstrated from the peaks of Sinai to the cliffs of Carmel. Our created world reveals His power and handiwork. He can turn stones into bread and bring water from rocks. He is powerful and He is good! God is there when we need Him!

The great angel chorus got it right! *"Glory to God in the highest, And on earth peace, goodwill toward men!"* and

"Holy, Holy, Holy, is the Lord God Almighty, who was and is and is to come!"

All tracks by G. R. Holton

To God Be The Glory!

1875

by Fanny J. Crosby

To God be the glory, great things he has done!
So loved he the world that he gave us his Son,
Who yielded his life an atonement for sin,
And opened the life gate that we may go in.

O perfect redemption, the purchase of blood!
To ev'ry believer the promise of God;
The vilest offender who truly believes,
That moment from Jesus forgiveness receives.

Great things he has taught us, great things he
has done,
And great our rejoicing through Jesus the Son;
But purer and higher and greater will be
Our wonder, our transport, when Jesus we see.

Refrain

Praise the Lord, praise the Lord,
Let the earth hear his voice!
Praise the Lord, praise the Lord,
Let the people rejoice!
O come to the Father thro' Jesus the Son,
And give him the glory, great things he has
done!

This song is unique from Crosby's other hymns because the words are wholly about God and His perfect glory, instead of *our praise* of Him.

We like to be in control and present our own image to the world, an image we seek to improve through any means possible.

On the other hand, there is great comfort in knowing that the image we try to make for ourselves doesn't matter.

We are made in the image of God, which means that whatever we do has to bring Him and Him alone glory. Our lives are wrapped up in God. It is all about HIM!

But what a joy and a comfort to know that though bad things may happen in our lives. God is ultimately in control.

God is still glorified even when the "vilest offender" believes.

While we should still try to live a holy and upright life, we should do so to bring God glory, not to ourselves.

Glory of God

Theme: *The Incomparable Almighty God*

2ND WEEK

INSIDE TRACK MEMORY VERSES	MIDDLE LANE SUPPORTING PASSAGES	FAST TRACK TOPICAL CHAPTERS
☐ **MONDAY** *O LORD, our Lord,* *how majestic is your name* *in all the earth!* Psalm 8:9	☐ **MONDAY** Psalm 29: 1-1-11 Psalm 145: 1-21 Psalm 148: 1-14	☐ **MONDAY** **Psalm 8**
☐ **TUESDAY** *And one cried unto another, and said,* *Holy, holy, holy, is Jehovah of hosts:* *the whole earth is full of his glory.* Isaiah 6:3 ASV	☐ **TUESDAY** Revelation 4: 5-5: 14 John 12: 37-50 John 1: 14-18	☐ **TUESDAY** **Isaiah 6**
☐ **WEDNESDAY** *. . a bright cloud overshadowed them . .* Matthew 17:5b ASV	☐ **WEDNESDAY** Mark 9: 2-9 Luke 9: 28-36 2 Peter 1: 16-19	☐ **WEDNESDAY** **Matthew 17**
☐ **THURSDAY** *Thou art worthy, O Lord, to receive glory and honor* *and power: for thou hast created all things, and for* *thy pleasure they are and were created.* Revelation 4:11 KJV	☐ **THURSDAY** Ezekiel 1: 22-28 1 Kings 22:19 Habakkuk 3: 1-7	☐ **THURSDAY** **Revelation 4**
☐ **FRIDAY** *And the city had no need of the sun, neither of the* *moon, to shine in it: for the glory of God did* *lighten it, and the Lamb is the light thereof.* Revelation 21:21 KJV	☐ **FRIDAY** Psalm 87: 1-3 Hebrews 12: 18-29 Ephesians 2: 13-22	☐ **FRIDAY** **Revelation 21**

QUESTION:
How can we see the glory of God?

ANSWER: The glory of God is more than just a feeling, an event about God, or only a bright shining light. The word "glory" means "heavy weight." It is the biggest, grandest thing about God. It is His presence and His power. The glory of God sets Him apart from all others as the all-powerful One! What does that mean to a common Christian?

If we look, we can see it now! How? By faith? Look up! The heavens "declare the glory of God." Look around you, "the firmament shows his handiwork." Stephen "gazed into heaven and saw the glory of God" while he was being stoned to death (Acts 7:55). The Ark of the Covenant was bathed in the "glory of God" called the *Shekinah*.

We will see it clearly later! Our present problems are "not worthy to be compared with the glory which shall be revealed in us" (Romans 8:18). Moses was given an earthly preview of it when he asked God, "Please show me your glory?" A full view is among the "riches of our inheritance" in eternity (Ephesians 1:17-18).

We currently walk in the Glory. The church is the temple of God and God dwells in us. What does that mean? "But we all, with unveiled face, beholding as in a mirror the glory of the Lord, are being transformed into the same image from glory to glory, just as by the Spirit of the Lord" (2 Corinthians 3:18, *NKJV*).

Middle Lane and Inside Track by Myra Anderson

Another Chapter from God's Book — 9th BIBLE READING MARATHON

This is My Father's World

1901

By Maltbie D. Babcockl 1858-1901

This is my Father's world,
And to my listening ears
All nature sings, and round me rings
The music of the spheres.
This is my Father's world:
I rest me in the thought
Of rocks and trees, of skies and seas–
His hand the wonders wrought.

This is my Father's world:
The birds their carols raise,
The morning light, the lily white,
Declare their Maker's praise.
This is my Father's world:
He shines in all that's fair;
In the rustling grass I hear Him pass,
He speaks to me everywhere.

This is my Father's world:
O let me ne'er forget
That though the wrong seems oft so strong,
God is the Ruler yet.
This is my Father's world:
Why should my heart be sad?
The Lord is King: let the heavens ring!
God reigns; let earth be glad!

This is My Father's World by Maltbie Davenport Babcock was published after his death in 1901. It was originally written as a poem containing sixteen verses of four lines each. Franklin L. Sheppard set the poem to music in 1915 and selected three verses for the final hymn.

Babcock, who was a minister from Lockport, New York, would often take walks overlooking a cliff, where he would enjoy the view of beautiful Lake Ontario and the upstate New York scenery. As he prepared to leave for his walks he would often tell his wife that he was "going out to see my Father's world."

Babcock depicts all nature rings in praise to God, including the birds, the morning sunlight and the white lilies. He believed that planets made music or harmony as they revolved around the Sun. Thus, his line "and round me rings the music of the spheres." Objects in space do in fact emit sounds similar to music.

The lyrics celebrate the wonderful world created by our Heavenly Father. The author sees the presence of God in it all, even "in the rustling of the grass" he heard God pass.

Yet, he did not want to forget that "though the wrong seems oft so strong" God is still the Ruler.

Creation is fallen and broken. Yet, it also still belongs to God. We must listen attentively to the voice of God in His world – physically; and we must hear his voice spiritually from His Word.

God's World

3RD WEEK

Theme: God's Spiritual and Worldly Universe

INSIDE TRACK MEMORY VERSES	MIDDLE LANE SUPPORTING PASSAGES	FAST TRACK TOPICAL CHAPTERS
☐ **MONDAY** *. . . it was very good.* Genesis 1:31 ESV	☐ **MONDAY** Proverbs 8:22-31 Psalm 8:3-4 Psalm 147:1-20	☐ **MONDAY** **Genesis 1**
☐ **TUESDAY** *Now the earth was corrupt in God's sight,* *and the earth was filled with violence.* Genesis 6:11 ESV	☐ **TUESDAY** Psalm 103 Deuteronomy 4:31-40 Isaiah 24:1-23	☐ **TUESDAY** **Genesis 6**
☐ **WEDNESDAY** *The heavens declare the glory of God, and* *the sky above proclaims His handiwork.* Psalm 19:1 ESV	☐ **WEDNESDAY** Psalm 96 Psalm 98 Psalm 104	☐ **WEDNESDAY** **Psalm 19**
☐ **THURSDAY** *How can a man be in the right before God?* Job 9:2b ESV	☐ **THURSDAY** Psalm 75 Isaiah 2:1-4 Micah 4:1-8	☐ **THURSDAY** **Job 9**
☐ **FRIDAY** *But according to His promise* *we are waiting for new heavens and a new earth* *in which righteousness dwells.* 2 Peter 3:13 ESV	☐ **FRIDAY** Jude:1-24 Isaiah 66:14-24 Genesis 7:1-24	☐ **FRIDAY** **2 Peter 3**

Growing Panes

QUESTION:

What does it mean, God is Creator?

ANSWER: The Bible introduces God, not with a list of attributes, but by describing an act: "In the beginning *God created* the heavens and the earth" (Genesis 1:1).

The dual realities of our existence on this planet are clearly revealed: the distinct difference between *the creator* and *the created*. God is *God*, and His creation (including man) is *the* act of God alone bringing into existence everything we call "our world." What does that mean?

God's ownership of all things is established. He is called Lord 7000 times in the Bible. "You are the LORD, you alone. You have made heaven, the heaven of heavens, with all their host, the earth and all that is on it, the seas and all that is in them; and you preserve all of them; and the host of heaven worships you" (Nehemiah 9:6). God's lordship includes His *control* over all things, His *authority* over all the universe, and His *presence* in every part of creation.

Creation granted God all authority. The right to tell all creatures (including the wind and the waves) what to do. "The LORD merely spoke, and the heavens were created. He breathed the word, and all the stars were born" (Psalm 33:6). Jesus, just a few days after his victory over the grave was granted "All authority" as Immanuel, God with us (Matthew 28:19).

God can be Everywhere as Creator. Creation is the basis of God's presence in all places of the universe at all times as He wills (Psalm 139). Our only response to God as Creator is to glorify His name and worship Him.

Middle Lane and Inside Track by Homer Anderson

Another Chapter from God's Book - 9th BIBLE READING MARATHON

What Can Wash Away My Sins?

1876

By Robert Lowry 1826-1899

What can wash away my sin?
Nothing but the blood of Jesus;
What can make me whole again?
Nothing but the blood of Jesus.

Refrain:
Oh! precious is the flow
That makes me white as snow;
No other fount I know,
Nothing but the blood of Jesus.

For my pardon this I see,
Nothing but the blood of Jesus;
For my cleansing this my plea,
Nothing but the blood of Jesus.

[Refrain]

Nothing can for sin atone,
Nothing but the blood of Jesus;
Naught of good that I have done,
Nothing but the blood of Jesus.

[Refrain]

This is all my hope and peace,
Nothing but the blood of Jesus;
This is all my righteousness,
Nothing but the blood of Jesus.

[Refrain]

Hebrews 9:22 was quoted underneath the title when this hymn was first published in 1876: *"Without the shedding of blood there is no remission of sin."*

This song elaborates on that idea, repeatedly stating that "nothing but the blood of Jesus" purifies us. The third stanza acknowledges that "naught of good that I have done" can save.

There were originally six stanzas, but typically only the first four are sung today. The two that are not used begin "Now by this I'll overcome" and "Glory! Glory! This I sing." The theme of the text is the redemptive work of Christ on the cross, seen through the image of His shed blood. The stanzas express the need for redemption from sin, and the matchless value of Jesus' redeeming blood.

As you sing the hymn, contemplate the significance of sin in separating us from God, and the great value of Jesus' work on the cross.

Condemned by Sin

4TH WEEK

Theme: **God Gave the World Up to Sin**

INSIDE TRACK MEMORY VERSES	MIDDLE LANE SUPPORTING PASSAGES	FAST TRACK TOPICAL CHAPTERS
☐ **MONDAY** *When the woman saw that the tree was good for food and pleasing to the eyes, and that it was desirable for obtaining wisdom, she took the fruit and ate it. She also gave some to her husband who was with her, and he ate it.* Genesis 3: 6 (BSB)	☐ **MONDAY** Genesis 2: 16-17 2 Corinthians 11: 3-4 Romans 5: 12-21	☐ **MONDAY** **Genesis 3**
☐ **TUESDAY** *This great dragon—the ancient serpent called the devil, or Satan, the one deceiving the whole world—was thrown down to the earth with all his angels.* Revelation 12: 9 (NLT)	☐ **TUESDAY** Job 1: 6-12 Matthew 4: 1-11 Revelation 20: 1-10	☐ **TUESDAY** **Revelation 12**
☐ **WEDNESDAY** *Although they know God's righteous decree that those who do such things are worthy of death, they not only continue to do these things, but also approve of those who practice them.* Romans 1: 32	☐ **WEDNESDAY** Genesis 6: 1-7 Matthew 24: 36–51	☐ **WEDNESDAY** **Romans 1**
☐ **THURSDAY** *But Samuel replied:* *Does the LORD delight in burnt offerings and sacrifices as much as in obeying the LORD? To obey is better than sacrifice, and to heed is better than the fat of rams.* 1 Samuel 15:22	☐ **THURSDAY** Mark 12: 28-34 Deuteronomy 6: 1-9 James 1: 19-27	☐ **THURSDAY** **1 Samuel 15**
☐ **FRIDAY** *With all my heart I have sought You; do not let me stray from Your commandments. I have hidden Your word in my heart that I might not sin against You.* Psalm 119: 10-11	☐ **FRIDAY** Psalm 51: 1-19 Psalm 1: 1-6	☐ **FRIDAY** **2 Samuel 11 & 12**

Growing Pains

QUESTION:

How do I sin?

ANSWER: The most common explanation for the concept of sin comes from the Greek word *hamartia*. It is translated "missing the mark" or "failure to reach a goal." The goal of life for a Christian is to do God's will, and you could do this by following the teachings and commands of the Bible in general, but the teachings of Jesus in particular. Christians have a covenant relationship with God to be obedient disciples of His Son, Jesus the Christ. Two distinct ways of sinning are found in the Scriptures:

We sin when we do the things God says to not do. These sins are usually called sins of *commission,* or when we do not observe the clear directives of God. Jesus said there are some things we must not do! This includes sexual immorality, impuri-ty, debauchery, idolatry, sorcery; hatred, discord, jealousy, rage, rivalries, divisions, factions, envy, drunkenness, orgies, and such like. Just to name a few such sins.

We sin when we omit to do the things God commands. These are sins of *omission.* Sins of omission are as easily identified as the sins of commission, but they are just as condemning as the former. The Scriptures conclude, "Therefore to him that knoweth to do good, and doeth it not, to him it is sin" (James 4:13–17). These acts of missing the mark are detailed in our failures to visit the sick, restore a brother, help the needy, study our Bibles, and such like.

Perhaps we should incorporate our knowledge of sin and the resistance to it into our everyday lives by seeking and maintaining a right <u>relationship with God</u>.

All Tracks by G. R. Holton

Another Chapter from God's Book - 9th BIBLE READING MARATHON

Higher Ground

by Johnson Oatman, Jr. 1856-1922

I'm pressing on the upward way,
New heights I'm gaining ev'ry day;
Still praying as I onward bound,
"Lord plant my feet on higher ground."

My heart has no desire to stay
Where doubts arise and fears dismay;
Tho' some may dwell where these abound,
My pray'r, my aim is higher ground.

I want to live above the world,
Tho' Satan's darts at me are hurl'd;
For faith has caught the joyful sound,
The song of saints on higher ground.

I want to scale the utmost height,
And catch a gleam of glory bright;
but still I'll pray till heav'n I've found,
"Lord lead me on to higher ground."

Chorus

Lord, lift me up and let me stand,
By faith on heaven's table land;
A higher plane than I have found,
Lord, plant my feet on higher ground.

This text by <u>Johnson Oatman Jr.</u> (1856–1922) and tune by <u>Charles H. Gabriel</u> (1856–1932) were written in 1892, when Oatman first started to write gospel songs and Gabriel had just moved to Chicago from California. Gabriel briefly recalled the experience later in life in his autobiography *Sixty Years of Gospel Song,* p. 10:

> In September, 1892, I reached Chicago, possessed of a wife, a six-moth-old son, a coat that buttoned up to the throat, a plug hat, a cane, and sixteen dollars in cash. At that time a book of songs for the Epworth League was being prepared by its secretary, Dr. J.F. Berry, who engaged me to assist him. Fortunately for the chattels above mentioned, my source of income was not delayed. . . .
>
> As a fact beyond my ability to understand, I never edited a book of songs that reimbursed me in royalties to the amount of money it cost me to gather the copy for the printer. On the other hand, every one I did compile produced one to five songs that proved successful. "Higher Ground" was one of the first I wrote after reaching Chicago. For it I received $5.00.

Many of Gabriel's songs came into common use among churches of Christ when he helped T. B. Larimore edit *The New Christian Hymn Book* in 1907 for the Gospel Advocate Co.

5th WEEK

True Worship

Theme: **Acceptable Worship in Spirit and Truth**

INSIDE TRACK *MEMORY VERSES*	MIDDLE LANE SUPPORTING PASSAGES	FAST TRACK TOPICAL CHAPTERS
☐ MONDAY *I appeal to you therefore, brothers, by the mercies of God, to present your bodies as a living sacrifice, holy and acceptable to God, which is your spiritual worship.* Romans 12: 1 ESV	☐ MONDAY Hebrews 13: 15-16 Proverbs 25: 21-22 Psalm 100: 1-5	☐ MONDAY Romans 12
☐ TUESDAY *God is spirit, and those who worship him must worship in spirit and truth.* John 4: 24 ESV	☐ TUESDAY Philippians: 3:3 Psalm 145: 18 1Timothy 2: 1-6	☐ TUESDAY John 4
☐ WEDNESDAY *Let the word of Christ dwell in you richly, teaching and admonishing one another in all wisdom, singing psalms and hymns and spiritual songs, with thankfulness in your hearts to God.* Colossians 3: 16 ESV	☐ WEDNESDAY Jeremiah 31: 31-34 2 Corinthians 5: 16-20 Hebrews 13: 20-21	☐ WEDNESDAY Hebrews 8
☐ THURSDAY *For though I am absent in body, yet I am with you in spirit, rejoicing to see your good order and the firmness of your faith in Christ.* Colossians 2: 5 ESV	☐ THURSDAY Romans 12: 6-8 1 Corinthians 14: 26-40 1 John 5: 1-6	☐ THURSDAY 1 Corinthians 14
☐ FRIDAY *Exalt the LORD our God; worship at His footstool! Holy is He!* Psalm 99: 5 ESV	☐ FRIDAY Psalm 107: 1 Psalm 100: 1-5 Exodus 15: 2	☐ FRIDAY Psalm 63 & 99

QUESTION:

How is True Worship Transforming?

ANSWER: Our goal is to be *transformed* into the image of Christ (Romans 12:1-2). This change occurs over time as we present our bodies as living sacrifices to Jesus in work and worship. How does worship transform us?

True worship is God-centered. Worship is to glorify and exalt God—to show our loyalty and admiration to our Father. Only He is worthy to be worshipped and not any of His servants (Revelation 19:10). Jesus tells us that true worshipers will worship God in spirit and in truth (John 4:24).

True worship is truth-based. To know the truth, to believe the truth, to hold convictions about the truth, and to love the truth will naturally result in true spiritual worship. We praise God for his mercies and by our obedience to His Word. Our worship must be rooted in and anchored by Biblical revelation. Christ-exalting worship must be doctrinally grounded and focused on the truth of our great God. Worship inconsistent with what is revealed to us in Scripture ultimately degenerates into false worship.

True worship is from the Heart. Worshipping God "in spirit" means that it must originate from within, from the heart; it must be sincere, motivated by our love for God and gratitude for all He is and has done for us. People who worship from the heart are deeply emotional. They have a strong love for God and the truth. Strong emotions for God that are rooted in truth compose the bone and marrow of true Biblical worship.

Middle Lane and Inside Track by Kevin Boyd

Another Chapter from God's Book - 9th BIBLE READING MARATHON

Holy, Holy, Holy

1826

by Reginald Heber 1783-1826

Holy, holy, holy! Lord God Almighty!
Early in the morning our song shall rise to thee.
Holy, holy, holy! Merciful and mighty!
God in three Persons, blessed Trinity!

Holy, holy, holy! All the saints adore thee,
casting down their golden crowns around the glassy sea;
cherubim and seraphim falling down before thee,
who wert, and art, and evermore shalt be.

Holy, holy, holy! Though the darkness hide thee,
though the eye of sinful man thy glory may not see,
only thou art holy; there is none beside thee
perfect in pow'r, in love, and purity.

Holy, holy, holy! Lord God Almighty!
All thy works shall praise thy name in earth
and sky and sea.
Holy, holy, holy! Merciful and mighty!
God in three Persons, blessed Trinity!

In 325 AD, Church leaders convened in the town of Nicaea in Bithynia to formulate a consensus of belief and practice amongst Christians.

What resulted was the Nicene Creed, a document passed on through the ages as one of the pillars of church doctrine. The primary function of this creed was to establish a firm belief in the Trinity, countering the heresy of Arius, who believed that Jesus was not fully divine.

It was this creed that inspired Reginald Heber to write this great hymn of praise to the Triune God, with the intent that the hymn be sung before or after the creed was recited in a service, and on Trinity Sunday – eight weeks after Easter.

The tune, composed by John B. Dykes for Heber's text, is also titled NICAEA in recognition of Heber's text.

The words evoke a sense of awe at the majesty of God, and call on all of creation – humans, saints and angels, and all living things – to praise the Godhead three-in-one.

Vain and False Worship

6TH WEEK

Theme: **Unacceptable and Idol Worship**

INSIDE TRACK MEMORY VERSES	MIDDLE LANE SUPPORTING PASSAGES	FAST TRACK TOPICAL CHAPTERS
☐ **MONDAY** *Not everyone who says to Me, 'Lord, Lord,' will enter the kingdom of heaven, but only he who does the will of My Father in heaven.* Matthew 7:21 BSB	☐ **MONDAY** Hebrews 2: 1-4 Hebrews 6: 1-12 Hebrews 10: 26-39	☐ **MONDAY** Jeremiah 7
☐ **TUESDAY** *For of this you can be sure: No immoral, impure, or greedy person (that is, an idolater), has any inheritance in the kingdom of Christ and of God.* Ephesians 5:5 NLT	☐ **TUESDAY** Isaiah 40: 18-34 1 Corinthians 8: 4-6 1 Corinthians 10: 14-22	☐ **TUESDAY** Jeremiah 10
☐ **WEDNESDAY** *They worship Me in vain; they teach as doctrine the precepts of men.* Mark 7:7 NIV	☐ **WEDNESDAY** Mark 7: 5-8 Galatians 1: 11-17 Colossians 2: 6-8, 16-23	☐ **WEDNESDAY** Matthew 15
☐ **THURSDAY** *God is spirit, and those who worship Him must worship in spirit and truth."* John 4:24 ESV	☐ **THURSDAY** Isaiah 44: 6-23 Romans 12: 1-2, 9-21	☐ **THURSDAY** Mark 7
☐ **FRIDAY** *He will exalt himself and defy everything that people call god and every object of worship. He will even sit in the temple of God, claiming that he himself is God.* 2 Thessalonians 2:4 NLT	☐ **FRIDAY** Matthew 24: 4-27 2 Thessalonians 2: 1-12 1 John 4:1-2	☐ **FRIDAY** Revelation 13

QUESTION:

Why is False Worship dangerous?

ANSWER: The problem with false worship is not an absence of sincerity in worship, but the absence of divine sanction. The problem is that such worship originates some place other than from God himself. False worshippers may be sincere, devoted, and sacrificial, but they do not have the approval of God.

__Appear dedicated and sacrificial.__ They often give liberally of their time and money. False worshippers may spend hours to gain converts. Their lifestyles may appear to maintain strict rules of righteousness. Sacrifice does not equal spirituality.

__Looks like True Worship.__ The acts of worship may be the same as those of true worshippers – prayers, praise, etc. Their intentions may be genuine, but good intentions do not equal true worship.

__Not authorized by God's Word.__ Scriptural authority is minimized. Unless we employ the written Word of God to define our worship, we risk offending God by using our opinions, traditions, or imagination for authority. Creativity is a wonderful gift; but we must not revel in new things that may contradict what God desires. We only know what God desires through his revelation to us, not our inventions or improvements.

May we pursue true worship as we look to the Word of God and worship according to all that he has revealed and prescribed in his divine revelation.

Middle Lane and Inside Track by Byron Brown

Another Chapter from God's Book - 9th BIBLE READING MARATHON

Praise the Lord, Ye Heavens Adore Him

1801

Anonymous

Praise the Lord! ye heav'ns adore him;
Praise him angels, in the height;
Sun and moon, rejoice before him;
Praise him, all ye stars of light.
Praise the Lord! for he has spoken;
Worlds his mighty voice obeyed;
Laws which never shall be broken
For their guidance he has made.

Praise the Lord! for he is glorious;
Never shall his promise fail;
God has made his saints victorious;
Sin and death shall not prevail.
Praise the God of our salvation!
Hosts on high his pow'r proclaim;
Heav'n, and earth, and all creation,
Laud and magnify his name.

Worship, honor, glory, blessing,
Lord, we offer unto thee;
Young and old, thy praise expressing,
In glad homage bend the knee.
All the saints in heav'n adore thee,
We would bow before thy throne;
As thine angels serve before thee,
So on earth thy will be done.

The text is often attributed to **John Kempthorne**, who was born at Plymouth, England, on June 24, 1775, the son of Admiral Kempthorne, and was educated at St. John's, Cambridge.

This hymn first appeared as one of five printed in a four-page tract, entitled *For Foundling Apprentices Attending Divine Service to Return Thanks*, which was in turn pasted at the end of a book called *Psalms, Hymns, and Anthems of the Foundling Hospital*, published in London, England.

It is found in both the music edition of 1796 and the words only edition of 1801, but is believed to have most likely been written in or after 1801 and pasted in both editions at the same time.

The Foundling Hospital, a London orphanage for deserted children, was established in 1739 by an English merchant sea-captain named Thomas Coram (1668-1751).

One Sunday morning, Coran was on his way to the church service at St. Andrew's in Holborn when he found an abandoned baby on the steps of the church building. This incident moved Coram to found an institution to care for the many illegitimate children in the city who suffered a similar fate.

So the hospital was built in High Holborn and had its own chapel, finished in 1750, where musical concerts were often given.

Hymn-singing by the inmates of charitable institutions was a well-established practice in the late eighteenth century. Such concerts, given as benefits for the orphanage, contributed greatly to its financial support over a period of many years, and it was quite a fashionable thing for Londoners to visit there, especially on Sundays.

- from https:*hymnstudiesblog.wordpress.com* a blog devoted to the study of the background, authors, composers, and meaning of hymns.

Praise and Prayer

Theme: **Bless the Lord, O My Soul**

INSIDE TRACK — MEMORY VERSES	MIDDLE LANE — SUPPORTING PASSAGES	FAST TRACK — TOPICAL CHAPTERS
☐ MONDAY *Sing praises to the LORD, for he has done gloriously; let this be made known in all the earth.* Isaiah 12:5 ESV	☐ MONDAY Psalms 34:1 Psalms 104:1-35 Ephesians 1:3-6	☐ MONDAY Psalm 103
☐ TUESDAY *But the path of the righteous is like the light of dawn, which shines brighter and brighter until full day.* Proverbs 4:18 ESV	☐ TUESDAY Psalms 8: 1-9 Joel 20: 26,27 Matthew 7: 11	☐ TUESDAY Psalm 84
☐ WEDNESDAY *And the glory of the LORD shall be revealed, and all flesh shall see it together, for the mouth of the LORD has spoken.* Isaiah 40:5 ESV	☐ WEDNESDAY Psalms 96: 1-13 Colossians 3: 1-4 2 Thessalonians 1: 5-12	☐ WEDNESDAY John 17
☐ THURSDAY *And all these blessings shall come upon you and overtake you, if you obey the voice of the LORD your God.* Deuteronomy 28:2 ESV	☐ THURSDAY Psalms 103: 1-22 Psalms 113: 1-9 Revelation 7: 9-12	☐ THURSDAY 1 Kings 8
☐ FRIDAY *So everyone who acknowledges me before men, I also will acknowledge before my Father who is in heaven.* Matthew 10:32 ESV	☐ FRIDAY Matthew 26: 47-56 Luke 23: 39-53 1 Corinthians 11: 23-32	☐ FRIDAY Mark 14

QUESTION:
How Does Prayer and Praise Help?

ANSWER: Prayer and praise make things happen for you and your circumstances because God's presence is welcomed and enthroned in your heart. God takes control. Paul and Silas had been severely beaten thrown into a dark, damp prison cell with no possible way of escape. They did not know what tomorrow would bring with no idea how long they would be there. But *"Around midnight Paul and Silas were* **praying and singing hymns to God,** *and the other prisoners were listening"* (Acts 16:25). What does praise and prayer do for us?

Deliver us from our Dark Prisons. Without praise we experience an eroding that leads to bondage and death. The Bible says, *"Although they knew God, they did not glorify Him as God, nor were thankful, but became futile in their thoughts, and their foolish hearts were darkened"* (Romans 1:21). We should replace our worries, our fears, our frustrations with praise. **God can turn our prison cells into a place of praise.**

Free us from Fear. It has been said that F-E-A-R stands for: F*alse* E*vidence* A*ppearing* R*eal.* The devil presents false evidence and makes it seem real. The prayer of praise defeats fear. God loves us. Praise Him for His great love. Remember, *"There is no fear in love; but perfect love casts out fear, because fear involves torment"* (1 John 4:18). God's love and fear cannot reside in the same heart!

Now is the time to lift a prayer of praise to God for everything in our lives. When we thank God, or when we give Him praise, that will start the process of receiving His Help!

Middle Lane and Inside Track by Janet Brown

Another Chapter from God's Book — 9ᵗʰ BIBLE READING MARATHON

When I Survey the Wondrous Cross

1707

By Isaac Watts 1674-1748

When I survey the wondrous cross
on which the Prince of glory died,
my richest gain I count but loss,
and pour contempt on all my pride.

Forbid it, Lord, that I should boast
save in the death of Christ, my God!
All the vain things that charm me most,
I sacrifice them through his blood.

See, from his head, his hands, his feet,
sorrow and love flow mingled down.
Did e'er such love and sorrow meet,
or thorns compose so rich a crown?

Were the whole realm of nature mine,
that were a present far too small.
Love so amazing, so divine,
demands my soul, my life, my all.

Regarding the final stanza of the song, Father Ignatius of St. Edmund's Church in London is reported to have blurted to the congregation: *"Well, I'm surprised to hear you sing that. Do you know that altogether you put only fifteen shillings in the collection bag this morning?"*

While Watts might not have been talking explicitly about money in the last line of his text, there is the expectation that we dedicate ourselves entirely to God, for God demands not just a piece of who we are, but "our soul, our life, our all."

This can be an incredibly difficult line to sing with any sense of honesty. Author Jerry Jenkins writes in his book *Hymns for Personal Devotions*, *"Perhaps it's the distance between where Watts encourages me to be and where I truly am that makes this hymn so hard to sing. It's a lofty and worthy spiritual goal to say that 'Love so amazing, so divine, demands my soul, my life, my all,' but how short I fall!"* (Jenkins, 44).

And so as we sing this hymn of love and awe, we must sing it with a prayer in our hearts, asking God to enable us each day to live our life wholly for him.

Giving to God

Theme: **Opening the Windows of Heaven**

8TH WEEK

INSIDE TRACK MEMORY VERSES	MIDDLE LANE SUPPORTING PASSAGES	FAST TRACK TOPICAL CHAPTERS
☐ MONDAY *give, and it will be given to you. . . pressed down, shaken together, running over, . . . with the measure you use it will be measured back to you.* Luke 6:38 ESV	☐ MONDAY 1 Corinthians 3:10-15 Deuteronomy 28:12 John 1:50-51	☐ MONDAY Malachi 3
☐ TUESDAY *Whoever has will be given more; whoever does not have, even what they have will be taken from them.* Mark 4:25 NIV	☐ TUESDAY Proverbs 28:20-28 Isaiah 65: 6-7 Matthew 7:2	☐ TUESDAY Luke 6
☐ WEDNESDAY *I beseech you . . . to present your bodies as a living sacrifice, holy and acceptable to God, which is your spiritual worship.* Romans 12:1 ESV	☐ WEDNESDAY Philippians 4:10 John 7: 14-19 Isaiah 41:10	☐ WEDNESDAY 1 Corinthians 16
☐ THURSDAY *For where your treasure is, there your heart will be also.* Matthew 6:21 ESV	☐ THURSDAY Acts 11:29-30 Philippians 4:19-20 Matthew 19:29-30	☐ THURSDAY 2 Corinthians 9
☐ FRIDAY *For my yoke is easy, and my burden is light.* Matthew 11:30 ESV	☐ FRIDAY John 14:15 Jeremiah 31:33 Revelation 3:20-21	☐ FRIDAY 1 John 5

QUESTION:
Should I, or Should I not Give?

ANSWER: Many Christians sit at the kitchen table with their bills, and they question whether they have money to give to the Lord. Jesus should settle this question with one statement: "... what do you benefit if you **gain** the world... but lose your soul" (Mark 8:36)? Yet, we are in a continuous battle with Satan over the question.

Concern vs. *Control:* We turn control over to God when we open our hearts to others. Giving takes the focus off ourselves and puts it onto someone or something else. Giving is a tangible way we can express concern for other people. The windows of heaven are then opened to us with blessings. Choosing not to give means not only robbing God but shutting the windows of heaven.

Contentment vs. *Covetousness:* Contentment means living with a sense of God's adequacy, a conviction that God is adequate for any need we face. Therefore, we can give joyfully, knowing God will supply our needs. We have joy in our lives, not because our purse is full, but because we have learned contentment.

Stewardship vs. *Stinginess:* God is the giver and landlord of everything. All that we own is a result of gracious gifts from God. Our mandate is to act as stewards and managers of God's resources. We all WANT to be a steward - God's servant. We should say to God: "I know this is all yours. You have entrusted it to me. I am managing it for you and for your kingdom. Here is the first fruits of my labor. Without You, none of this would be possible."

Money is a bad master, but a good servant! Remembering that will help me to determine whether I am God's servant - his steward of all He has entrusted to me, OR whether I have the attitude of Owner.

Middle Lane and Inside Track by Jerry Deloach

Another Chapter from God's Book - 9th BIBLE READING MARATHON

GREAT IS THY FAITHFULNESS

1923

By Thomas O. Chisholm 1866-1960

Great is thy faithfulness, O God my Father.
There is no shadow of turning with thee.
Thou changest not, thy compassions,
they fail not.
As thou hast been thou forever wilt be.

Refrain:
Great is thy faithfulness!
Great is thy faithfulness!
Morning by morning new mercies I see.
All I have needed thy hand hath provided.
Great is thy faithfulness, Lord, unto me!

Summer and winter, and springtime and harvest,
sun, moon, and stars in their courses above,
join with all nature in manifold witness
to thy great faithfulness, mercy, and love.
[Refrain]

Pardon for sin and a peace that endureth,
thine own dear presence to cheer and to guide,
strength for today and
bright hope for tomorrow;
blessings all mine, with ten thousand beside!
[Refrain]

Thomas Chisholm, the author of "Great Is Thy Faithfulness" led a pretty ordinary life. He did not write this hymn during a period of intense grief or after encountering God in a profound way.

Instead, he found truth in the words he encountered in Lamentations 3:22-23: *"Because of the LORD's great love we are not consumed, for his compassions never fail. They are new every morning; great is your faithfulness."*

Jeremiah, on the other hand, was in tumultuous circumstances when writing Lamentations. The people to whom he prophesied did not listen, and he was ostracized and completely alone because of what God called him to do.

He also lamented the consequences of their *faithlessness.* God allowed them to be conquered by the Babylonians, resulting in their entire world being laid to waste.

But in the midst of that utter devastation, Jeremiah still offers them hope on the horizon: they are not completely destroyed because of the LORD's compassion and faithfulness, and in the morning, after this "dark night of the soul," things will be better.

So whether we are at a place in our lives where everything is pretty ordinary, or whether we are in a period of grief: no matter what our circumstances, God never changes and is faithful to us, sustaining us in his compassion and faithfulness each and every day.

God's Faithfulness

9TH WEEK

Theme: *Be Faithful for God is Faithful*

INSIDE TRACK MEMORY VERSES	MIDDLE LANE SUPPORTING PASSAGES	FAST TRACK TOPICAL CHAPTERS
MONDAY *Make every effort to live in peace with everyone and to be holy; without holiness no one will see the Lord.* Hebrews 12: 14 NIV	**MONDAY** Deuteronomy 8: 1-9 1 Peter 1: 9-12 Hebrews 6: 13-20	**MONDAY** Hebrews 12
TUESDAY *Nevertheless, God's solid foundation stands firm, sealed with this inscription: "The Lord knows those who are his," and, "Everyone who confesses the name of the Lord must turn away from wickedness.* 2 Timothy 2: 19 NIV	**TUESDAY** Colossians 3: 12-17 Luke 22: 39-46 Ephesians 1:11-14	**TUESDAY** 2 Timothy 2
WEDNESDAY *Let us examine our ways and test them, and let us return to the LORD.* Lamentations 3: 40 NIV	**WEDNESDAY** Psalm 32: 1-11 Luke 15: 11-24 Matthew 21: 28-32	**WEDNESDAY** Lamentations 3
THURSDAY *Blessed are the pure in heart, for they will see God.* Matthew 5:8 NIV	**THURSDAY** 1 Samuel 2: 1-10 1 Corinthians 10: 6-13 Psalm 4: 4-8	**THURSDAY** Psalm 24
FRIDAY *God made him who had no sin to be sin for us, so that in him we might become the righteousness of God.* 2 Corinthians 5:21 NIV	**FRIDAY** Romans 1: 6-17 Revelations 21: 1-8 Galatians 6: 1-10	**FRIDAY** 2 Corinthians 5

Growing Panes

QUESTION:

Are God's mercies new every morning?

ANSWER: The faithfulness of God is celebrated by Jeremiah (Lamentations 3:22-23) at a low time in the history of God's people. The great city of Jerusalem had just fallen into the hands of Babylon (586 BC) and there was great anguish and pain.

Amid that pain, Jeremiah instills hope by reminding them of the "steadfast love of the Lord" and proclaiming, *"The Lord's mercies...are new every morning: great is thy faithfulness."*

We are reminded of the unfailing mercy of God that gives us hope. *Mercy* is God's withholding of a just punishment we deserve.

Isaiah (63:7) expressed it like this: *"I will tell of the LORD's unfail-*

ing love. I will praise the LORD for all he has done. I will rejoice in his great goodness to Israel, which he has granted according to his mercy and love."

The Lord has pity on His suffering children; in fact, His mercies are *new every morning*.

The dawning of every new day is a symbol of God's light breaking through the darkness and His mercy overcoming our troubles. Every morning demonstrates God's grace, a new beginning in which gloom must flee. We need look no further than the breath in our lungs, the sun that shines upon us, or the rain that falls to nourish the soil. All these proclaim, "Great is thy faithfulness, thy mercies endure forever!"

There is no expiration date on God's mercy toward us. Like the manna in the wilderness, His mercies are new every morning and always available to those in need.

Middle Lane and Inside Track by Ruth Harrison

Another Chapter from God's Book - 9th BIBLE READING MARATHON

He Leadeth Me, O Blessed Thought

1862

By Joseph H. Gilmore 1834-1918

He leadeth me: O blessed thought!
O words with heavenly comfort fraught!
Whate'er I do, where'er I be,
still 'tis God's hand that leadeth me.

Refrain:
He leadeth me, he leadeth me;
by his own hand he leadeth me:
his faithful follower I would be,
for by his hand he leadeth me.

2 Sometimes mid scenes of deepest gloom,
sometimes where Eden's flowers bloom,
by waters calm, o'er troubled sea,
still 'tis God's hand that leadeth me.
Refrain

3 Lord, I would clasp thy hand in mine,
nor ever murmur nor repine;
content, whatever lot I see,
since 'tis my God that leadeth me.
Refrain

4 And when my task on earth is done,
when, by thy grace, the victory's won,
e'en death's cold wave I will not flee,
since God through Jordan leadeth me.
Refrain

Joseph Gilmore was preaching at a mid-week prayer service on the topic of Psalm 23 when this song was birthed. He wrote later,

"I set out to give the people an exposition of the 23rd Psalm, but I got no further than the words 'He leadeth me.' Those words took hold of me as they had never done before. I saw in them a significance and beauty of which I had never dreamed...At the close of the meeting a few of us kept on talking about the thoughts which I had emphasized; and then and there, on a back page of my sermon notes, I penciled the hymn just as it stands today, handed it to my wife, and thought no more of it...She sent it without my knowledge to the Watchman and Reflector magazine, and there it first appeared in print December 4, 1862" (Psalter Hymnal Handbook, 616).

Like the psalm after which this hymn was written, the verses declare our trust in God, wherever we are – whether in stormy seas, Eden's garden, or on death's door. Each verse provides a different scenario in which we need God to guide us, and the refrain acts as a response in which we profess that God does guide us and will be our Shepherd at all times.

It is amazing what we can learn when we take time to listen and ponder God's Word.

God leads us in every aspect of our lives, including our worship of Him.

Servant-Leaders for Christ

10TH WEEK

Theme: **Do as I have done...Pick Up Your Towel!**

INSIDE TRACK MEMORY VERSES	MIDDLE LANE SUPPORTING PASSAGES	FAST TRACK TOPICAL CHAPTERS
☐ **MONDAY** *For even the Son of Man did not come to be served, but to serve, and to give his life as a ransom for many.* Mark 10: 45 NIV	☐ **MONDAY** Philippians 2: 3-11 1 Peter 2: 21-23 John 18: 28-40	☐ **MONDAY** Isaiah 53
☐ **TUESDAY** *Therefore, I urge you, brothers and sisters, in view of God's mercy, to offer your bodies as a living sacrifice, holy and pleasing to God--this is your true and proper worship.* Romans 12: 1 NIV	☐ **TUESDAY** Philippians 2: 19-24 2 Corinthians 8: 1-5 Romans 10: 11-15	☐ **TUESDAY** Acts 4, 11, 13
☐ **WEDNESDAY** *Submit to one another out of reverence for Christ.* Ephesians 5: 21 NIV	☐ **WEDNESDAY** Colossians 3: 18-24 Romans 12: 9-21 1 Corinthians 10: 23-11	☐ **WEDNESDAY** Hebrews 13
☐ **THURSDAY** *This is how we know what love is: Jesus Christ laid down his life for us. And we ought to lay down our lives for our brothers and sisters.* 1 John 3: 16 NIV	☐ **THURSDAY** Philippians 2: 25-29 Romans 16: 1-4 1 Peter 4: 7-11	☐ **THURSDAY** Acts 6, 7
☐ **FRIDAY** *Remind the people to be subject to rulers and authorities, to be obedient, to be ready to do whatever is good, to slander no one, to be peaceable and considerate, and always to be gentle toward everyone.* Titus 3: 1-2 NIV	☐ **FRIDAY** Romans 14: 15-18 James 5: 13-20 Colossians 3: 12-17	☐ **FRIDAY** John 13

QUESTION:
Who wants to be first?

ANSWER: Our world thrives on possessing authority and power. "Achievement" is not always the road to becoming leaders, but traditional wisdom suggests that we all desire to be the best, the most successful, to be first! Why? Because first in line means influence, prestige, position...power! Leaders.

By way of contrast, servants are on the opposite end of this tandem. They are there for the benefit of others. Jesus taught that greatness and power are not measured by how many people are under a leader, but by the extent that the leader is serving those under his/her leadership. True greatness, true leadership, *being first* is achieved in giving oneself in selfless service to the followers. Servant-leaders are defined by two traits: they *serve* and *lead* others. Christians are called to motivate others to make major changes in their lives...that's leadership! The lack of leadership produces followers who are "like sheep without a shepherd" (Matthew 9:36). In God's kingdom, leaders serve us best by *leading us* and lead best by *serving us*.

Jesus again turns the world upside down. Leaders must serve, and servants must lead! Wow! Who wouldn't rather be a leader than a servant?

The short answer is this:

> *"...if anyone wants to be first, he must be the very last and the servant of all"* (Mark 9:34).

Middle Lane and Inside Track by Kenny Holton

Trust and Obey

1887

By John H. Sammis 1846-1919

When we walk with the Lord
in the light of his word,
what a glory he sheds on our way!
While we do his good will,
he abides with us still,
and with all who will trust and obey.

Refrain:
Trust and obey, for there's no other way
to be happy in Jesus, but to trust and obey.

Not a burden we bear,
not a sorrow we share,
but our toil he doth richly repay;
not a grief or a loss,
not a frown or a cross,
but is blest if we trust and obey.

[Refrain]

But we never can prove
the delights of his love
until all on the altar we lay;
for the favor he shows,
for the joy he bestows,
are for them who will trust and obey.

[Refrain]

Then in fellowship sweet
we will sit at his feet,
or we'll walk by his side in the way;
what he says we will do,
where he sends we will go;
never fear, only trust and obey.

[Refrain]

John H. Sammis wrote the refrain and then the stanzas of this hymn after being inspired by a friend.

A friend, Daniel Towner, was present at an evangelistic meeting in Brockton, Massachusetts where he heard a young man who responded say, "*I am not quite sure –but I am going to trust, and I am going to obey.*"

This impressed the friend, and he wrote these words down and sent it to Sammis with the story of the young man.

Sammis wrote the chorus lines first and then the five stanzas, after which Towner composed the tune.

This hymn paints a picture of communion with God in which fear and gloom have disappeared, and delight and joy saturate one's existence.

However, this attractive life is not free – the Christian must totally surrender control of his life to God, and commit to trusting obedience to God's will, as the final stanza says – "what He says we will do, where He sends we will go."

Jesus said, "Take my yoke upon you, and learn from me, for I am gentle and lowly in heart, and you will find rest for your souls. For my yoke is easy, and my burden is light." (Matthew 11:29-30 ESV).

11TH WEEK

Disbelief and Disobedience

Theme: Deny Ungodliness and Worldly Lust

INSIDE TRACK MEMORY VERSES	MIDDLE LANE SUPPORTING PASSAGES	FAST TRACK TOPICAL CHAPTERS
MONDAY *And Moses said, Wherefore now do ye transgress the commandment of the LORD? but it shall not prosper.* Numbers 14: 41 KJV	**MONDAY** Numbers 13: 16-25 Numbers 14: 5-12 Numbers 9: 25-28	**MONDAY** Numbers 13, 14
TUESDAY *Jesus said unto him, If you can believe, all things are possible to him that believes.* Mark 9: 23 KJV	**TUESDAY** Mark 9: 25-29 Romans 1: 18-20 1 John 2:14-17	**TUESDAY** Mark 9
WEDNESDAY *You shall have no other gods before me.* Exodus 20: 3 KJV	**WEDNESDAY** Deuteronomy 28: 1-6 Deuteronomy 28: 14-19 Deuteronomy 28: 58-63	**WEDNESDAY** Deuteronomy 28
THURSDAY *But He said, "The things that are impossible with people are possible with God."* Luke 18: 27 KJV	**THURSDAY** Romans 11: 26-30 Luke 18: 22-26 Jude 16-17	**THURSDAY** Luke 18
FRIDAY *But put on the Lord Jesus Christ, and make no provision for the flesh, to gratify its desires.* Romans 13:14 ESV	**FRIDAY** Titus 1: 12-16 Titus 2: 11-14 Titus 3: 1-7	**FRIDAY** Titus 1,2, 3

QUESTION:
Who are the ungodly?

ANSWER: People who are "ungodly" are separated from God. Their lives are polluted with sin and disobedience to God. These people act in a way that is incongruent with the nature of God. *They actually oppose God!*

The evil desires of the flesh, and the acts that come from such desires, are acts of ungodliness. Ultimately, those who reject God—the ungodly—will be separated from Him forever (Revelation 20:14-15).

False teachers are ungodly. Jude describes characteristics of ungodliness: they pervert the grace of God into a license for immorality, and they deny Jesus Christ as the only Sovereign and Lord (Jude 1:4). They are characterized as *"grumblers and faultfinders"* who selfishly follow *"their own evil desires,"* boast and flatter (verse 16). The ungodly scoff at the truth of God and attempt to divide churches (verses 18–19).

However, Jesus died for the ungodly (Romans 5:6-8). The ungodly are justified and saved by the righteousness of God through Christ (Romans 4:5). As Christians, we strive *"to walk in a manner worthy of the Lord, fully pleasing to him: bearing fruit in every good work and increasing in the knowledge of God"* (Colossians 1:10).

More specifically, the ungodly are those who do not know God through His Son Jesus Christ. Believers in Christ strive to remove all ungodliness from their lives (1 John 3:9) and live godly lives.

Middle Lane and Inside Track by John Hunt

Another Chapter from God's Book - 9th BIBLE READING MARATHON

Blessed Assurance, Jesus is Mine

By Fanny Crosby 1820-1915

Blessed assurance, Jesus is mine!
Oh, what a foretaste of glory divine!
Heir of salvation, purchase of God,
born of his Spirit, washed in his blood.

Refrain:
This is my story, this is my song,
praising my Savior all the day long.
This is my story, this is my song,
praising my Savior all the day long.

Perfect communion, perfect delight,
visions of rapture now burst on my sight.
Angels descending bring from above
echoes of mercy, whispers of love.

[Refrain]

Perfect submission, all is at rest.
I in my Savior am happy and bless'd,
watching and waiting, looking above,
filled with his goodness, lost in his love.

[Refrain]

Fanny Crosby was blind. The joy of this hymn may be focused in one phrase in the second stanza: *"visions of rapture now burst on my sight."*

This phrase speaks of things being right with the world. It is a testimony of faith in the coming world prepared for faithful saints.

Heaven will be a place where the deaf would hear and the blind receive their sight. This is a stanza that reminds us that God is preparing a world in righteousness and making all things new. What a vision of beauty that will be!

Ira Sankey, good friend of hymn author Fanny Crosby, once related this story about the comfort "Blessed Assurance" provides:

> "'During the recent war in the Transvaal,' said a gentleman at my meeting in Exeter Hall, London, in 1900, 'when the soldiers going to the front were passing another company whom they recognized, their greetings used to be, "Four-nine-four, boys; four-nine-four;" and the salute would invariably be answered with "Six further on, boys; six further on."
>
> The significance of this was that, in 'Sacred Songs and Solos,' a number of copies of the small edition of which had been sent to the front, number 494 was 'God be with you till we meet again'; and six further on than 494, or number 500, was 'Blessed Assurance, Jesus is mine'" (*My Life and Sacred Songs*, 69).

From the very day she wrote them, Crosby's words have provided comfort for millions of Christians in the face of fear, persecution, sorrow, and doubt.

In spite of all the trials that may come, we know that we serve a Savior who came to bring the Kingdom of God on earth, and as we serve Him, we participate in, and belong to, that Kingdom. We each play our own part in that "glorious foretaste" of what is still to come. We belong to Christ and his Kingdom – what an assurance this is!

Practices of Righteousness

12ᵀᴴ WEEK

Theme: *Things That Pertain to Life and Godliness*

INSIDE TRACK — MEMORY VERSES	MIDDLE LANE — SUPPORTING PASSAGES	FAST TRACK — TOPICAL CHAPTERS
MONDAY *Therefore, dear friends, let us purify ourselves from everything that contaminates body and spirit, perfecting holiness out of reverence for God.* 2 Corinthians 7:1 NIV	**MONDAY** 2 Timothy 3:16-17 Romans 3:21-26 2 Corinthians 7:1	**MONDAY** 2 Peter 1
TUESDAY *Nothing impure will ever enter it, nor will anyone who does what is shameful or deceitful, but only those whose names are written in the Lamb's book of life.* Revelation 21:27 NIV	**TUESDAY** 2 Peter 2:7-9 1 Peter 1:7 Psalm 16:27	**TUESDAY** James 3
WEDNESDAY *If you really know me, you will know my Father as well. From now on, you do know him and have seen him.* John 14:7 NIV	**WEDNESDAY** Revelation 22:15 Proverbs 14:15 Colossians 1: 9-12	**WEDNESDAY** Philippians 3
THURSDAY *For God, who said, "let light shine out of darkness," made His light shine in our hearts to give us the light of the knowledge of God's glory displayed in the face of Christ.* 2 Corinthians 4:6 NIV	**THURSDAY** Revelation 3:20 John 3:29 Malachi 3:16	**THURSDAY** 1 John 1
FRIDAY *By faith we understand that the universe was formed at God's command, so that what is seen was not made out of what was visible.* Hebrews 11:3 NIV	**FRIDAY** Genesis 5:21-24 Joshua 6:22-25 2 Peter 3:5-7	**FRIDAY** Hebrews 11

QUESTION:

What is Godliness with Contentment?

ANSWER: Christians live *in the world* but must *not be worldly!* Seeking worldly goods, becoming wealthy, is what many seek, including some Christians. Paul warned, *"To them, a show of godliness is just a way to become wealthy"* (1 Timothy 6:5b).

The Bible does not say that it is wrong to be rich. But *"where your treasure is, your heart will be also"* (Matthew 6:21). The rich are commanded *"not to be arrogant nor to put their hope in wealth"* (1 Timothy 6:17).

But it is impossible to be content when our hearts are set on gaining more of this world's goods. We will not remain godly for long if we are not content with what God has given us. A desire for godliness is quickly eroded by a greedy, covetous spirit.

Rather than consider amassing wealth as great gain, the Bible says, "godliness with contentment is great gain."

Paul told Timothy to "flee from all this [eagerness to get rich], and pursue righteousness, godliness, faith, love, endurance and gentleness" (1 Timothy 6:11).

Christians must pursue holiness in conduct, attitude, and thought. We must choose to be content in whatever circumstances God has given us if we want to be truly content in godly living.

The difference is in the heart. Both greed and contentment are states of the heart. Choose to be content with the riches of Christ (Colossians 1:27; Ephesians 3:8).

Middle Lane and Inside Track by Marilyn King

It is Well with My Soul

1873

By Horatio Gates Spafford   1828-1888

When peace like a river attendeth my way,
when sorrows like sea billows roll;
whatever my lot, thou hast taught me to say,
"It is well, it is well with my soul."

Refrain:
It is well with my soul;
it is well, it is well with my soul.

Though Satan should buffet, though trials should come,
let this blest assurance control:
that Christ has regarded my helpless estate,
and has shed his own blood for my soul.

Refrain

My sin oh, the bliss of this glorious thought!
my sin, not in part, but the whole,
is nailed to the cross, and I bear it no more;
praise the Lord, praise the Lord,
O my soul!

Refrain

O Lord, haste the day
when my faith shall be sight,
the clouds be rolled back as a scroll;
the trump shall resound and
the Lord shall descend;
even so, it is well with my soul.

Refrain

Horatio Spafford sent his wife and four daughters in November, 1873 on the French ship *Ville du Havre* from their home in Chicago to a vacation in France, planning to join them a few days later.

Somewhere in the Atlantic, the *Ville du Havre* collided with a British ship coming the other way, and sank.

Of his family, only Spafford's wife survived. His four daughters perished.

Spafford took the next boat over, and as he passed the spot where the ship went down, began to write, *"When peace like a river attendeth my way, when sorrows like sea billows roll,"* and continued until he had the text, *"It is well with my soul."*

Perhaps what is most startling about this text is the first line: "When peace like a river attendeth my way." What does that mean, "peace like a river?"

Lisa McKay addresses the question beautifully when she says, "I used to think of peace primarily as a stillness – a pause, a silence, a clarity – but that sort of peace is not the peace of rivers.

There is a majestic, hushed sort of calm to rivers, but they are not silent and they are certainly not still – even the most placid of rivers is going somewhere...I've stopped expecting peace to look like the pristine silence that follows a midnight snowfall. I'm coming to appreciate a different sort of peace instead – a peace that pushes forward, rich with mud, swelling and splashing and alive with the music of water meeting rock." (McKay, "Peace Like a River," *rachelheldevans.com*)

All of our own sufferings will one day be removed through the suffering of Christ and the power of the cross. We are reminded of this by this song.

New Beginnings

Theme: ...Again! Starting Over!

13ᵀᴴ WEEK

INSIDE TRACK MEMORY VERSES	MIDDLE LANE SUPPORTING PASSAGES	FAST TRACK TOPICAL CHAPTERS
☐ MONDAY *Then he threw his arms around his brother Benjamin and wept, and Benjamin embraced him weeping. And he kissed all his brothers and wept over them.* Genesis 45:14-15 NIV	☐ MONDAY Malachi 3: 17-18 Proverbs 29: 3 Matthew 18: 12-14	☐ MONDAY Luke 15
☐ TUESDAY *Give ear and come to me; listen, that you may live. I will make an everlasting covenant with you.* Isaiah 55:3 NIV	☐ TUESDAY Isaiah 54: 8-9 Matthew 24: 35-39 Hebrews 13: 20-21	☐ TUESDAY Genesis 8, 9
☐ WEDNESDAY *And whatever you do, whether in word or deed, do it all in the name of the Lord Jesus, giving thanks to God the Father through him.* Colossians 3:17 NIV	☐ WEDNESDAY Romans 11: 1-6 James 5: 7-9 Romans 9: 27-29	☐ WEDNESDAY 1 Kings 18, 19
☐ THURSDAY *Yet he was merciful; he forgave their iniquities and did not destroy them. Time after time he restrained his anger and did not stir up his full wrath.* Psalm 78:38 NIV	☐ THURSDAY James 1: 13-15 1 Corinthians 9: 24-27 Proverbs 28: 13-14	☐ THURSDAY 2 Samuel 11, 12
☐ FRIDAY *David said about him: I saw the Lord always before me. Because he is at my right hand, I will not be shaken.* Acts 2:25 NIV	☐ FRIDAY 2 Corinthians 1: 12 Matthew 13: 40-43 Acts 2: 22-28	☐ FRIDAY 1 Corinthians 15

QUESTION:
How do we begin again?

ANSWER: Three times in God's plan of salvation opportunities are provided for new beginnings. His plan is to free his creation from the ravaging wrath of sin and death. Snatching us from the grip of the Devil!

First, to enter the Kingdom of God. Jesus told Nicodemus that *"unless one is born of water and the spirit he could not enter the Kingdom of God"* (John 3:3).

On the Day of Pentecost (Acts 2) three thousand entered the Kingdom of God when the Word of God cut them to their hearts. In their conversion they turned from their sins, washed them away in baptism (Acts 22:16) and started a new life as a child of God. They were born again of water and spirit. Souls were translated from the kingdom of darkness to the kingdom of light.

Second, to return from sin. The prodigal son who returned to the mires of sin after being born in the father's house *"came to himself"* and returned home (Luke 15). He confessed his sin and asked to be accepted back into the family. He was given a second chance to begin again.

Third, to be saved from death. Our resurrections from death will be the final opportunity for new beginnings (1 Corinthians 15). The final words of the final book of inspiration welcome the faithful into a *"new heaven and a new earth"* of righteousness (Revelation 21-22).

On these occasions God's grace and His mercy prompt Him to reach out with His Love to us as sinners, offering us new beginnings. Why? Because God does *"not want anyone to perish, but everyone to come to repentance"* (2 Peter 3:9)!

Middle Lane and Inside Track by John King

Another Chapter from God's Book - 9th BIBLE READING MARATHON

On Jordan's Stormy Banks I Stand

1787

By Samuel Stennett

On Jordan's stormy banks I stand,
and cast a wishful eye
to Canaan's fair and happy land,
where my possessions lie.

Refrain:
I am bound for the promised land,
I am bound for the promised land;
oh, who will come and go with me?
I am bound for the promised land.

O'er all those wide extended plains
shines one eternal day;
there God the Son forever reigns,
and scatters night away.

[Refrain]

No chilling winds or poisonous breath
can reach that healthful shore;
sickness and sorrow, pain and death,
are felt and feared no more.

[Refrain]

When I shall reach that happy place,
I'll be forever blest,
for I shall see my Father's face,
and in his bosom rest.

[Refrain]

Jesus came to earth to complete God's plan of redemption from sin. He died on the cross, was raised to life again, and went back to heaven to prepare a place for his disciples.

Before His resurrection, Jesus proclaimed his clarion call to make new disciples: *"Go, make disciples of all nations, baptizing them into the name of the father, the son, and the holy spirit" (Matthew 28:19-20).*

In Revelation, the apostle John describes his vision of heaven and the new Jerusalem which is the end of the gospel message.

Not only is it a beautiful place, "prepared as a bride adorned for her husband" (Rev. 21:2 ESV), with pearls, gold, and jewels, but it is also a place of joy and light. "He [God] will wipe away every tear from their eyes, and death shall be no more, neither shall there be mourning, nor crying, nor pain anymore" (Rev. 21:4 ESV). "And night will be no more. They will need no light of lamp or sun, for the Lord God will be their light, and they will reign forever and ever" (Rev. 22:5 ESV).

Images like these are expressed in this hymn, along with the desire to be there someday. This hymn is evangelistic. This hymn clearly sings about life after the storms of life.

Seeking the Lost

14TH WEEK

Theme: **Come Unto Me, I Will Give You Rest**

INSIDE TRACK MEMORY VERSES	MIDDLE LANE SUPPORTING PASSAGES	FAST TRACK TOPICAL CHAPTERS
☐ MONDAY *Arise, go to Nineveh, that great city, and preach to it the message that I tell you.* Jonah 3:2 NKJV	☐ MONDAY Isaiah 40:3-5 Luke 3:2-3 Luke 4:17-19	☐ MONDAY Jonah 1,2, 3
☐ TUESDAY *Go therefore and make disciples of all the nations…* Matthew 28:19a NKJV	☐ TUESDAY Mark 1:7-8, 14-15 Mark 3:13-14 Mark 8:34-37	☐ TUESDAY Matthew 10, 28
☐ WEDNESDAY *And it shall come to pass that whoever calls on the name of the Lord shall be saved.* Acts 2:21 NKJV	☐ WEDNESDAY Joel 2:28-32 Psalm 16:8-11 Psalm 110:1-4	☐ WEDNESDAY Acts 2
☐ THURSDAY *Therefore those who were scattered went everywhere preaching the word.* Acts 8:4 NKJV	☐ THURSDAY Romans 6:3-4 Colossians 2:12 I Peter 3:18-22	☐ THURSDAY Acts 8, 9
☐ FRIDAY *..for all have sinned and fall short of the glory of God.* Romans 3:23 NKJV	☐ FRIDAY Ecclesiastes 7:20 Psalm 14:1-3 Ephesians 2:1-10	☐ FRIDAY Romans 3

QUESTION:
Are we all going to Heaven by different roads?
ANSWER: Jesus said, *"I am the way and the truth and the life. No one comes to the Father except through Me"* (John 14:6). There is no other path to heaven! No other way to the Father. Peter taught this same truth to the rulers in Jerusalem, saying about Jesus, *"Salvation is found in no one else, for there is no other name under heaven given to men by which we must be saved"* (Acts 4:12). The exclusive nature of the only path to salvation is expressed in the words of Jesus, *"I am the way."*

In these words, Jesus declared Himself to be the *only path* to heaven, the *only true* measure of righteousness, and the *only source* of life now and spiritual life for eternity.

Such an exclusive statement may confuse, surprise, or even offend, but it is true nonetheless. The Bible clearly teaches that there is no other way to salvation except through Jesus Christ.

It is *His Way* or no way!

That "way" (path, road, route) was how Jesus went back to Heaven and how his followers would also get there. Jesus took the road of faith in His Father and faithful obedience, even to death! That road was clearly marked in the Gospel His disciples preached (Matthew 28:18-20). Faith and obedience to Jesus, God's only begotten Son.

The "only road" to heaven is narrow! Most people choose to take the broader freeways whose destinations are *not* to Heaven.

Middle Lane and Inside Track by John Klimko

Another Chapter from God's Book - 9th BIBLE READING MARATHON

Encamped Along the Hills of Light

1891

By John Henry Yates, 1837– 1900

Encamped along the hills of light,
Ye Christian soldiers, rise
And press the battle ere the night
Shall veil the glowing skies.
Against the foe in vales below
Let all our strength be hurled;
Faith is the victory, we know,
That overcomes the world.

Chorus:
Faith is the victory! (Faith is the victory!)
Faith is the victory! (Faith is the victory!)
Oh, glorious victory
That overcomes the world.

His banner over us is love,
Our sword the Word of God;
We tread the road the saints above
With shouts of triumph trod.
By faith they, like a whirlwind's breath,
Swept on o'er ev'ry field;
The faith by which they conquered death
Is still our shining shield.

[Chorus]

To him who overcomes the foe
White raiment shall be giv'n;
Before the angels he shall know
His name confessed in heav'n.
Then onward from the hills of light,
Our hearts with love aflame;
We'll vanquish all the hosts of night
In Jesus' conq'ring name.

[Chorus]

John Henry Yates (1837-1900) was a lay minister in the Methodist Church and author of several popular poems and hymn lyrics.

At the age of 18 Yates entered the family business, a shoe store, in order to support his parents.

Ira Sankey, who composed the music, apparently came into contact with Yates's writing through a reprint of his popular sentimental poem "The Model Church," one of his "old man" songs in which the protagonist describes his joy in finding a modern church with the old-time religion.

"Faith is the Victory" is by far Yates's most successful gospel song, and is one of the most successful of all Sankey's compositions as well. It is still quite popular among the Churches of Christ having been introduced as early as the 1921 *Great Songs of the Church*.

This hymn is about the continuing battle between righteousness and unrighteousness! Good and evil! What is right and what is wrong! The stanzas stand out as pep talks to the troops before the battle begins.

The simple refrain drives home the point: *"Faith is the victory that overcomes the world."* Yates quotes here from 1 John 5:4, *"For everyone who has been born of God overcomes the world. And this is the victory that has overcome the world--our faith."*

Sincere faith motivates obedience to God in all things, "obtaining the outcome of your faith, the salvation of your souls" (1 Peter 1:9).

May we continue to "wage the good warfare" of faith (1 Timothy 1:18), and "let us hold fast the confession of our hope without wavering, for He who promised is faithful" (Hebrews 10:23).

-from http://drhamrick.blogspot.com/

Victory in Christ

15TH WEEK

Theme: *Understanding the Greatness of God's Powers*

INSIDE TRACK — MEMORY VERSES	MIDDLE LANE SUPPORTING PASSAGES	FAST TRACK TOPICAL CHAPTERS
☐ **MONDAY** *But the Helper, the Holy Spirit, whom the Father will send in my name, he will teach you all things and bring to your remembrance all that I have said to you.* John 14: 26 ESV	☐ **MONDAY** Acts 2: 38 Isaiah 55: 1-4 Psalm 107: 8-9	☐ **MONDAY** Romans 8
☐ **TUESDAY** *He said to me: "It is done. I am the Alpha and the Omega, the Beginning and the End. To the thirsty I will give water without cost from the spring of the water of life.* Revelation 21: 6 NIV	☐ **TUESDAY** 1 Corinthians 6: 14-17 John 6: 35-39 Isaiah 40: 28-29	☐ **TUESDAY** Isaiah 55
☐ **WEDNESDAY** *He gives his king great victories; he shows unfailing kindness to his anointed, to David and his descendants forever.* 2 Samuel 22: 51 NIV	☐ **WEDNESDAY** Matthew 12: 18-21 1 Corinthians 15: 57-58 1 John 5: 1-4	☐ **WEDNESDAY** Psalm 44
☐ **THURSDAY** *But let him ask in faith, with no doubting, for the one who doubts is like a wave of the sea that is driven and tossed by the wind.* James 1: 6 ESV	☐ **THURSDAY** Jude 20-21 1 Corinthians 1: 4-6 Romans 1: 1-6	☐ **THURSDAY** John 20
☐ **FRIDAY** *Your servant is here among the people you have chosen, a great people, too numerous to count or number.* 1 Kings 3: 8 NIV	☐ **FRIDAY** Colossians 3: 12-15 I Peter 2: 9-10 Deuteronomy 14: 1-2	☐ **FRIDAY** Ephesians 1

QUESTION:

Why will we win against Satan?

ANSWER: Christians battle every day against the forces of evil. We do not fight against flesh and blood, but against "spiritual wickedness in high places." Life-defeating, joy-stealing, salvation-depriving attacks challenge our defenses and threaten our faith in God. In Romans 8 Paul reminds us that not only will we win in the end, but that Jesus also enables us to win now.

The short answer is simple: we will win because we are more than able to stand against Satan because God holds us in His love.

Just a few historical answers state this fact: (Exodus 14:14) *"The Lord will fight for you, you need only to be still and know that He is God";* (Jeremiah 1:19) *"They. . . will not overcome you, for I am with you and will rescue you".*

Ultimately, Paul states it best (Romans 8:37-39 BSB) *"No, in all these things we are more than conquerors through Him who loved us. For I am convinced that neither death nor life, neither angels nor principalities, neither the present nor the future, nor any powers, neither height nor depth, nor anything else in all creation, will be able to separate us from the love of God that is in Christ Jesus our Lord."*

When we face the enemy and the temptations he hurls at us, we are not alone! Whether on our own dark mountains of despair or in the valleys of evil, we fight with confidence knowing God fights with us. Nothing the Devil does gives him the power to "snatch" us from the grip of God's love. We win because Christ is on our side!

We are more than conquers through Christ!

Middle Lane and Inside Track by Carrie Seat

Our God, Our Help in Ages Past

1719

By Isaac Watts 1674-1748

O God, our help in ages past,
our hope for years to come,
our shelter from the stormy blast,
and our eternal home;

Under the shadow of your throne
your saints have dwelt secure.
Sufficient is your arm alone,
and our defense is sure.

Before the hills in order stood,
or earth received its frame,
from everlasting you are God,
to endless years the same.

A thousand ages in your sight
are like an evening gone,
short as the watch that ends the night
before the rising sun.

Time, like an ever-rolling stream,
soon bears us all away.
We fly forgotten, as a dream
dies at the op'ning day.

O God, our help in ages past,
our hope for years to come,
still be our guard while troubles last,
and our eternal home.

Isaiah 41:9-10 says,

"I took you from the ends of the earth, from its farthest corners I called you. I said, 'You are my servant'; I have chosen you and have not rejected you. So do not fear, for I am with you; do not be dismayed, for I am your God. I will strengthen you and help you; I will uphold you with my righteous right hand."

No matter our situation, no matter our struggles and fears, no matter doubts, we are told to have courage, for the Lord is our God. And as Isaac Watts writes so powerfully in this hymn, our God is everlasting, and will be our help through all of our years.

The first verse gives us every assurance we need: God is our help, our hope, and our home. This does not blithely dismiss our fears and troubles. They are, and always will be, very real. But it does assure us that even if we cannot feel the immediate comfort, or even when all we can do is lament, we have a God that withstands the storms of the life and the tests of time, and who protects us and hears our cries.

This text was written by Isaac Watts in 1714, shortly before the death of Queen Anne of England. This was a time of great crises and turmoil, as the successor of Queen Anne was as yet undetermined, and the fear of a monarch who would reinstate the persecution of Protestants was great.

King George I prevented such persecution, but the fear before Anne's death was great. This was the context in which Watts wrote his powerful text, now lauded as "one of the grandest in the whole realm of English Hymnody" (Bailey, *The Gospel in Hymns*, 54).

God Provides

Search Me, O God, and Know My Heart

16ᵀᴴ WEEK

INSIDE TRACK MEMORY VERSES	MIDDLE LANE SUPPORTING PASSAGES	FAST TRACK TOPICAL CHAPTERS

☐ **MONDAY**

"*Before I formed you in the womb I knew you, before you were born I set you apart; I appointed you as a prophet to the nations.*"
Jeremiah 1: 5 NIV

☐ **TUESDAY**

Accordingly, though I am bold enough in Christ to command you to do what is required, yet for love's sake I prefer to appeal to you—I, Paul, an old man and now a prisoner also for Christ Jesus
Philemon 1: 8-9 ESV

☐ **WEDNESDAY**

But God removed Saul and replaced him with David, a man about whom God said, 'I have found David son of Jesse, a man after my own heart. He will do everything I want him to do.'
Acts 13: 22 NLT

☐ **THURSDAY**

You, Solomon my son, know the God of your father and serve him with a whole heart and with a willing mind, for the LORD searches all hearts and understands every plan and thought.
1 Chronicles 28: 9a ESV

☐ **FRIDAY**

God sent him to buy freedom for us who were slaves to the law, so that he could adopt us as his very own children.
Galatians 4: 5 NLT

MIDDLE LANE

☐ MONDAY
Isaiah 55: 6-9
Hebrew 4: 12-13
Luke 1: 50-51

☐ TUESDAY
Acts 13: 1-3
Acts 22: 3-16
I Timothy 1: 12-14

☐ WEDNESDAY
Acts 13: 36-37
Romans 4: 4-8
Psalm 9: 1-6

☐ THURSDAY
Psalm 22: 4-5
Isaiah 25: 9
Jerimiah 17: 7-8

☐ FRIDAY
Ephesians 1: 3-10
Romans 9: 6-9
Acts 27: 30-35

FAST TRACK

☐ MONDAY
Psalm 139

☐ TUESDAY
Acts 26

☐ WEDNESDAY
1 Samuel 17

☐ THURSDAY
Esther 3, 4

☐ FRIDAY
Romans 11

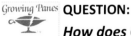 **QUESTION:**

How does God provide for us?

ANSWER: Short answer: *by searching our hearts!* When God searches our hearts, he examines how genuine *our actions* are and *He understands* the anxieties and pressures we face.

David prayed, "*Search me, God, and know my heart; test me and know my anxious thoughts. See if there is any offensive way in me and lead me in the way everlasting*" (Psalm 139: 23-24).

David knew firsthand how God provides. When Jesse's son, Eliab, appeared to be the most logical candidate to become King, David the youngest was selected. Why? God told Samuel, "*Do not consider his appearance or height, for I have re-* jected him; the LORD does not see as man does. For man sees the outward appearance, but the LORD sees the heart.*" (1 Samuel 16:7, BSB).

When God looked at the heart of David, He saw a man after His own heart (Acts 13:22). God sees what people cannot see!

God investigates our hearts. "*The eyes of the LORD search the whole earth in order to strengthen those whose hearts are fully committed to him*" (2 Chronicles 16:9).

Like Samuel, we can't see what the Lord sees. We can trust that, when God looks at our hearts, He sees our faithfulness, our true character, and our value as individuals. He knows our motivation and purposes. Then, He gives us _what we need_ ... not necessarily what we want!

A Mighty Fortress is Our God

1529

By Martin Luther   1483-1546

A mighty fortress is our God,
a bulwark never failing;
our helper he, amid the flood
of mortal ills prevailing.
For still our ancient foe
does seek to work us woe;
his craft and power are great,
and armed with cruel hate,
on earth is not his equal.

Did we in our own strength confide,
our striving would be losing,
were not the right Man on our side,
the Man of God's own choosing.
You ask who that may be?
Christ Jesus, it is he;
Lord Sabaoth his name,
from age to age the same;
and he must win the battle.

And though this world, with devils filled,
should threaten to undo us,
we will not fear, for God has willed
his truth to triumph through us.
The prince of darkness grim,
we tremble not for him;
his rage we can endure,
for lo! his doom is sure;
one little word shall fell him.

That Word above all earthly powers
no thanks to them abideth;
the Spirit and the gifts are ours
through him who with us sideth.
Let goods and kindred go,
this mortal life also;
the body they may kill:
God's truth abideth still;
his kingdom is forever!

This hymn is often referred to as "the battle hymn" of the Reformation. Many stories have been relayed about its use.

Albert Bailey writes, "*It was, as Heine said, the Marseillaise of the Reformation...It was sung in the streets...It was sung by poor Protestant emigres on their way to exile, and by martyrs at their death...Gustavus Adolphus ordered it sung by his army before the battle of Leipzig in 1631...Again it was the battle hymn of his army at Lutzen in 1632...It has had a part in countless celebrations commemorating the men and events of the Reformation; and its first line is engraved on the base of Luther's monument at Wittenberg...An imperishable hymn! Not polished and artistically wrought but rugged and strong like Luther himself, whose very words seem like deeds*" (The Gospel in Hymns, 316).

The text is not restricted, however, to times of actual physical battles. In any time of need, when we do battle with the forces of evil, God is our fortress to hide us and protect us, and the Word that endures forever will fight for us.

Luther wrote this text sometime between 1527 and 1529 as a paraphrase of Psalm 46, though stanza four comes directly from Luther's own persecution experience.

The most commonly used English version is a translation by Frederick H. Hedge in 1853.

The text may be understood in terms of a spiritual struggle against the powers of darkness. Whether we believe in very real, physical demons and tempters, or less concrete forces, we are in the midst of a very real war between good and evil. Luther reminds us that we can't simply sit back and watch as horrible things unfold in our world, but that we must join the battle, knowing that God is on our side.

God's Protection

17TH WEEK

Theme: *Be Strong in the Lord and the Power of His Might*

INSIDE TRACK
MEMORY VERSES

☐ MONDAY

In all your ways acknowledge him,
and he will make straight your paths.
Proverbs 3:6 NIV

☐ TUESDAY

I call upon the LORD,
who is worthy to be praised,
and I am saved from my enemies.
Psalm 18:3 NIV

☐ WEDNESDAY

Now to him who is able to do far more abundantly
than all that we ask or think,
according to the power at work within us.
Ephesians 3:20 NIV

☐ THURSDAY

The angel of the LORD
encamps around those who fear him,
and he delivers them.
Psalm 34:7 NIV

☐ FRIDAY

Submit yourselves, then, to God.
Resist the devil, and he will flee from you.
James 4:7 NIV

MIDDLE LANE
SUPPORTING PASSAGES

☐ MONDAY
Joshua 1:5-9
2 Chronicles 14:9-12
Isaiah 54:14-17

☐ TUESDAY
2 Samuel 22:29-36
Deuteronomy 6:16-25
Colossians 1:9-13

☐ WEDNESDAY
1 Peter 5:6-11
Isaiah 61:1-7
Romans 8:31-39

☐ THURSDAY
1 Samuel 17:31-37
2 Peter 2:4-9
Hebrews 12:22-24

☐ FRIDAY
2 Chronicles 20:15-17
Luke 21:29-36
Philippians 3:7-21

FAST TRACK
TOPICAL CHAPTERS

☐ MONDAY
Ephesians 6

☐ TUESDAY
Psalm 91

☐ WEDNESDAY
2 Corinthians 4

☐ THURSDAY
Exodus 14

☐ FRIDAY
Nahum 1

QUESTION:
How Does God Protect us?

ANSWER: God promised the Israelites that He would protect them if they obeyed His commandments (Leviticus 25:18–19). God would keep them physically safe.

The Hebrew word translated "safety" means *"a place of refuge; security, trust, confidence, hope."* God's protection for His people is recorded from the events like the flood to the deliverance of all the prophets. God kept them safe from their enemies...if they obeyed his commandments.

In the journeys of the Apostle Paul several examples of God physically protecting him are recorded (Acts 9:25; 17:10; 19:30; 23:10). Yet, Jesus and the New Testament writers focused more on spiritual safety. Spiritual protection from eternal death only found in one place—faith in the shed blood of Christ and obedience to Him! This is where Christians' faith resides... in "a place of refuge; security, trust, confidence, hope!"

Unfortunately, many are deceived into thinking that true security is provided by the things of the world—money, comforts, position, or power. But the safety these things provide is temporary and fleeting.

But, we do not "fear" physical insecurity. Jesus said, **"And do not fear those who kill the body but cannot kill the soul. Rather fear him who can destroy both soul and body in hell** (Matthew 10:28). We can be in great danger in this world of physical harm and still have the spiritual security of assurance in Christ.

Middle Lane and Inside Track by Toni Webb

Blest Be the Tie that Binds

1792

By John Fawcett 1740-1817

Blest be the tie that binds
our hearts in Christian love;
the fellowship of kindred minds
is like to that above.

Before our Father's throne
we pour our ardent prayers;
our fears, our hopes, our aims are one,
our comforts and our cares.

We share our mutual woes,
our mutual burdens bear,
and often for each other flows
the sympathizing tear.

When we are called to part,
it gives us inward pain;
but we shall still be joined in heart,
and hope to meet again.

This glorious hope revives
our courage by the way;
while each in expectation lives
and waits to see the day.

From sorrow, toil, and pain,
and sin, we shall be free;
and perfect love and friendship reign
through all eternity.

A popular though somewhat unreliable story about the writing of this hymn states:

" In 1772 Fawcett was completing his service to a small church in Wainsgate, England, having accepted a call to a larger congregation in London. However, after he had preached his farewell sermon and loaded the carts for the move, the tearful entreaties of his congregation persuaded him to stay in Wainsgate, where he ministered for the rest of his life. This hymn is supposed to have been written in response to this experience."

This hymn begins by stating that the body of Christ is bound together by love. The second and third stanzas of this hymn elaborate on the idea of suffering and rejoicing together, and the hymn concludes with the hope that this unity will not be permanently broken by death or parting. These themes are found in a lengthy passage in one of Paul's letters. He closed a short section on the unity and diversity of the body of Christ with this thought: "If one member suffers, all suffer together; if one member is honored, all rejoice together. Now you are the body of Christ and individually members of it" (1 Cor. 12:26-27 ESV). A few verses later, he began the great chapter on love (1 Cor. 13).

In the first three stanzas the author speaks of the strength of the bond of Christian love, and its practical implications that Christians must pray for and actively support one another.

Although the hymn was written about the binding love of fellow Christians, it would certainly include the love between a Christian husband and wife. The Apostle Paul makes this analogy in Ephesians 5.

Sacredness of Marriage

18ᵀᴴ WEEK

Theme: *God Joins a Man and Woman in Marriage*

INSIDE TRACK MEMORY VERSES	MIDDLE LANE SUPPORTING PASSAGES	FAST TRACK TOPICAL CHAPTERS
☐ MONDAY *For this reason a man will leave his father and mother and be united to his wife, and the two will become one flesh?* Matthew 19:5 NLT	☐ MONDAY Mark 10:3-9 Ephesians 5:21-33 I Corinthians 7:10-11	☐ MONDAY **Matthew 5, 19**
☐ TUESDAY *But I say that a man who divorces his wife, unless she has been unfaithful, causes her to commit adultery. And anyone who marries a divorced woman also commits adultery.* Matthew 5:32 NLT	☐ TUESDAY Leviticus 20:9-12 Deuteronomy 24:1-5 John 8:5	☐ TUESDAY **Deut. 22, 24**
☐ WEDNESDAY *Go show love to your wife again, though she is loved by another and is an adulteress. Love her as the LORD loves the Israelites, though they turn to other gods and offer raisin cakes to idols.* Hosea 3:1b BSB	☐ WEDNESDAY Jeremiah 3:1-3 Hosea 4:1-5 Jeremiah 4:1-2	☐ WEDNESDAY **Hosea 1,2, 3**
☐ THURSDAY *But there is one thing I want you to know: The head of every man is Christ, the head of woman is man, and the head of Christ is God.* 1 Corinthians 11:3 NLT	☐ THURSDAY Matthew 19:5 Genesis 3:16 Genesis 2:18-24	☐ THURSDAY **Ephesians 5**
☐ FRIDAY *Husbands, love your wives and never treat them harshly.* Colossians 3:19 NLT	☐ FRIDAY 1 Peter 3:7 Romans 13:8-10 Luke 16:18	☐ FRIDAY **1 Corinthians 7**

QUESTION:
What about Same-Sex Marriage?

ANSWER: The Bible does not directly address the question of gay/same sex marriage. However, *homosexuality* is explicitly condemned in both the Old Testament and the New Testament. The clear prohibition says, *"You shall not lie with a male as with a woman; it is an abomination* (Leviticus 18:22). The Apostle Paul (Romans 1:26–27) declares homosexual desires and actions to be "shameful" and "unnatural." To the church in Corinth the inspired Scripture says, *"Or do you not know that the unrighteous will not inherit the kingdom of God? Do not be deceived: neither the sexually immoral, nor idolaters, nor adulterers, nor men who practice homosexuality* (1 Corinthians 6:9).

According to the Bible, marriage is ordained by God as the lifetime union of a man and a woman (Genesis 2:21–24; Matthew 19:4–6). This truth is also found in every human civilization in world history. History argues against gay marriage. Modern secular psychology recognizes that men and women are psychologically and emotionally designed to complement one another.

Since the practice of homosexuality is condemned in the Bible, it follows that homosexual marriage is not God's will and would be, in fact, sinful.

As Christians, we cannot condone nor ignore sin. But, as ministers of reconciliation, we must share the love of God to all sinners (2 Corinthians 5:18). We must tell of the forgiveness of sins through Jesus Christ available to all of us.

We must speak the truth in love (Ephesians 4:15) and contend for truth with *"gentleness and respect"* (1 Peter 3:15).

Middle Lane and Inside Track by Ronnie West

Another Chapter from God's Book - 9ᵗʰ BIBLE READING MARATHON

I Surrender All

1896

By Judson W. Van DeVenter 1855-1939

All to Jesus I surrender,
All to Him I freely give;
I will ever love and trust Him,
In His presence daily live.

Refrain:
I surrender all, I surrender all;
All to Thee, my blessed Savior,
I surrender all.

All to Jesus I surrender,
Make me, Savior, wholly Thine;
Let me feel Thy Holy Spirit,
Truly know that Thou art mine.

[Refrain]

All to Jesus I surrender,
Lord, I give myself to Thee;
Fill me with Thy love and power,
Let Thy blessing fall on me.

[Refrain]

Judson W. Van De Venter was a painter turned evangelist who wrote this hymn in 1896. He said that it was written "in memory of the time when, after a long struggle, I had surrendered and dedicated my life to active Christian service. The song was written while I was conducting a meeting …"

The hymn originally had five stanzas, but the last is usually omitted (the second line is "Now I feel the sacred flame").

The theme of the hymn is the qualities that total surrender to God requires: free choice, humility, desire for relationship, and an attitude of reception toward God's blessings. The refrain and the first line of each stanza repeat the statement of commitment – "I surrender."

It is human nature to seek power and accomplishment through conflict, hence the popularity of athletic contests. Defeat in a championship game is humiliating, and giving up is even more so.

Christ calls His followers to totally surrender themselves to Him. He described it this way: "Or what king, going out to encounter another king in war, will not sit down first and deliberate whether he is able with ten thousand to meet him who comes against him with twenty thousand? And if not, while the other is yet a great way off, he sends a delegation and asks for terms of peace. So therefore, any one of you who does not renounce all that he has cannot be my disciple." (Luke 14:31-33 ESV)

Freedom in Serving God

Theme: *In Matters of Faith and Opinion*

19th WEEK

INSIDE TRACK MEMORY VERSES	MIDDLE LANE SUPPORTING PASSAGES	FAST TRACK TOPICAL CHAPTERS
MONDAY *Therefore, as we have opportunity, let us do good to all people, especially to those who belong to the family of believers.* Galatians 6:10 NIV	**MONDAY** Ephesians 2:1-10 Romans 12:1-21 Matthew 21:42-44	**MONDAY** 1 Peter 2
TUESDAY *Take my yoke upon you, and learn from me, for I am gentle and lowly in heart, and you will find rest for your souls. For my yoke is easy, and my burden is light.* Matthew 11:29-30 ESV	**TUESDAY** Isaiah 40:25-31 Ephesians 4:1-16 Hebrews 4:1-3	**TUESDAY** Matthew 11
WEDNESDAY *I know and am convinced by the Lord Jesus that there is nothing unclean of itself; but to him who considers anything to be unclean, to him it is unclean.* Romans 14:14-15 NKJV	**WEDNESDAY** Romans 16:17-27 1 Corinthians 2:1-16 1 Corinthians 10:14-33	**WEDNESDAY** Romans 14
THURSDAY *For Scripture says, "Do not muzzle an ox while it is treading out the grain," and "The worker deserves his wages."* 1 Timothy 5:18 NIV	**THURSDAY** Mark 7:18-23 Acts 15:12-22 Numbers 18:20-32	**THURSDAY** 1 Corinthians 8,9
FRIDAY *Be watchful, stand firm in the faith, act like men, be strong. Let all that you do be done in love.* 1 Corinthians 16:13-14 ESV	**FRIDAY** 1 Chronicles 22:9-16 Romans 15:1-16 Matthew 6:1-20	**FRIDAY** Joshua 1

Growing Panes **QUESTION:**

Do We Live in Freedom, or Slavery?

ANSWER: "Freedom," especially in America, is the highest virtue. It is clearly defined in our national Bill of Rights in matters of speech, religion and eight other "inalienable rights."

We value our freedom! But the Bible tells us that, spiritually speaking, no one is free (Romans 6), we are all slaves! We are either slaves to sin or slaves to righteousness. It depends on who you obey.

Christians are slaves of Christ, but truly free! For *"If the Son sets you free, you will be free indeed"* (John 8:36). The Apostle Paul explained, *"Through Christ Jesus the law of the Spirit of life set me free from the law of sin and death"* (Romans 8:2).

Christians know the truth and that truth sets us free (John 8:32). In addition, because of our bondage to Christ, we have also become sons and heirs of God (Galatians 4:1–7).

If you are in Christ, you have real "inalienable rights." Due to your new birth, you have a new status as a slave for Christ to faithfully obey Him. His power is yours to *"not let sin reign in your mortal body so that you obey its evil desires"* (Romans 6:12).

A man carried a chest-placard on the streets of New York City that read: "I AM A SLAVE FOR CHRIST." When he passed, the placard on his back read, 'WHOSE SLAVE ARE YOU?'

Freedom or slavery? Both!

Middle Lane and Inside Track by Leon Weeks

Another Chapter from God's Book - 9th BIBLE READING MARATHON

Break Thou the Bread of Life

1880

By Mary A. Lathbury 1841-1913

Break thou the bread of life, dear Lord, to me,
as once you broke the loaves beside the sea.
Beyond the sacred page I seek you, Lord;
my spirit waits for you, O living Word.

Bless your own word of truth, dear Lord, to me,
as when you blessed the bread by Galilee.
Then shall all bondage cease, all fetters fall;
and I shall find my peace, my All in all!

You are the bread of life, dear Lord, to me,
your holy word the truth that rescues me.
Give me to eat and live with you above;
teach me to love your truth, for you are love.

O send your Spirit now, dear Lord, to me,
that he may touch my eyes and make me see.
Show me the truth made plain within your Word,
for in your book revealed I see you, Lord.

Mary Lathbury authored the words to this hymn. She often wrote hymns to accompany various parts of the Bible.

Eventually known as the "Poet of Chautauqua," Lathbury was seen as a kind and gentle Christian soul whose creativity was immense. "Break Thou the Bread of Life," is one of her two most widely known hymns.

Many have been misled in thinking that this hymn is a reference to the Lord's Supper, when it is actually centered upon studying God's word. This hymn can be seen in reference to John 6:35 which reads, "And Jesus said unto them, I am the bread of life: he that cometh to me shall never hunger; and he that believeth in me shall never thirst."

In some hymnals, the third and fourth stanzas are omitted and the text is modernized.

This hymn has served as both a comfort and inspiration to many people since its first publication. Before every mid-week service, the great English preacher G. Campbell Morgan would read the words to this hymn to help him focus on his message. The primary focus of this hymn is centered upon Bible study and the desire to glean truth from God's word.

Spiritual Food

20TH WEEK

Theme: *Food That Satisfies Our Spiritual Desires*

INSIDE TRACK — MEMORY VERSES	MIDDLE LANE SUPPORTING PASSAGES	FAST TRACK TOPICAL CHAPTERS
MONDAY Jesus answered, "It is written: 'Man shall not live on bread alone, but on every word that comes from the mouth of God.'" Matthew 4:4 NIV	**MONDAY** Deuteronomy 8:1-18; 2 Corinthians 3:3-6; Isaiah 55:1-3	**MONDAY** 1 Kings 17
TUESDAY Put on the full armor of God, so that you can take your stand against the devil's schemes. Ephesians 6:11 NIV	**TUESDAY** Colossians 1:10-11; Romans 8:1-17; 2 Timothy 1:7-10	**TUESDAY** Galatians 5
WEDNESDAY Then Jesus declared, "I am the bread of life. whoever comes to me will never go hungry, and whoever believes in me will never be thirsty. John 6:35 NIV	**WEDNESDAY** Matthew 6:28-34; Revelation 3:20-21; Psalm 107:1-9	**WEDNESDAY** John 6
THURSDAY Blessed are those who hunger and thirst for righteousness, for they will be filled. Matthew 5:6 NIV	**THURSDAY** Hebrews 5:12-14; Acts 2:40-42; Psalm 81:10-16	**THURSDAY** 1 Corinthians 10,11
FRIDAY For the Lord watches over the way of the righteous, but the way of the wicked leads to destruction Psalm 1:6 NIV	**FRIDAY** John 15:2-6; 1 Corinthians 15:50-58; Galatians 5:22-25	**FRIDAY** Psalm 1

 **QUESTION:** *What is spiritual food?*

ANSWER: *"Eat the Book?"* …that is what John was told to do (Revelation 10:1-10)! Jesus said, *"Most assuredly, I say to you, unless you eat the flesh of the Son of Man and drink His blood, you have no life in you"* (John 6:53).

Spiritual food is *not* physical! The food we are talking about comes from the Spirit of God…*and* it is the only source of life - Eternal life. That food comes to us from God in *"words"* (John 6:63).

Like physical food, the "words" of God are not something merely read but must be "eaten" by God's people. We read the Word, but we then pause to "chew on it" a while, meditating and reflecting on the meaning and then we apply what we've read to our lives (see Psalm 1:1–3).

The Bible describes spiritual food as milk (1 Peter 2:2), meat (1 Corinthians 3:2) and bread (John 6). It is usually sweet like honey (Psalm 119:103) but may also be bitter (Revelation 10:9). The apostle Paul said, *"Preach the word! Be ready in season and out of season. Convince, rebuke, exhort, with all longsuffering and teaching"* (2 Timothy 4:2). We take in both the sweet and the bitter!

The prophet Jeremiah wrote, *"When your words came, I ate them; they were my joy and my heart's delight, for I bear your name, LORD God Almighty"* (Jeremiah 15:16).

Jesus clearly answers this question, *"My food is to do the will of him who sent me and to accomplish his work"* (John 4:34, ESV). We, too, need to "eat" the Word of God to have strength to accomplish His work.

Oh, Holy Night

1847

By Placide Cappeau 1808-1877

O holy night! the stars are brightly shining;
It is the night of the dear Savior's birth.
Long lay the world in sin and error pining,
Till He appeared and the soul felt its worth.
A thrill of hope- the weary world rejoices,
For yonder breaks a new and glorious morn!
Fall on your knees! O hear the angel voices!
O night divine, O night when Christ was born!
O night, O holy night, O night divine!

Led by the light of faith serenely beaming,
With glowing hearts by His cradle we stand.
So led by light of a star sweetly gleaming,
Here came the Wise Men from Orient land.
The King of kings lay thus in lowly manger,
In all our trials born to be our Friend.
He knows our need— to our weakness is no stranger.
Behold your King, before Him lowly bend!
Behold your King, before Him lowly bend!

Truly He taught us to love one another;
His law is love and His gospel is peace.
Chains shall He break, for the slave is our brother,
And in His name all oppression shall cease.
Sweet hymns of joy in grateful chorus raise we;
Let all within us praise His holy name.
Christ is the Lord! O praise His name forever!
His pow'r and glory evermore proclaim!
His pow'r and glory evermore proclaim!

Placide Cappeau was licensed to practice law in 1831. Instead, he became a merchant of wines and spirits, but his focus was really on literature.

A parish priest in Cappeau's community, asked him to write a Christmas poem, and he agreed to do it, despite being an avowed atheist and vocal anti-cleric.

He researched the book of Luke and wrote the lyrics to "O Holy night".

An opera singer, Emily Laurie, saw the text and asked a Jewish friend of hers to compose music for it, which he, remarkably, did. She sung it at a midnight mass three weeks later, and parishioners raved, but when Catholic church leaders found out it was written by an atheist, they banned it. However, its popularity only grew.

A side story: In 1906 Reginald Fessenden, a 33 year-old university professor and former chief chemist for Thomas Edison, did something thought impossible. Using a new type of generator, he spoke into a microphone and for the first time in history a voice was broadcast over the airwaves.

He read, from the book of Luke, *"And it came to pass in those days, that a decree went out from Caesar Augustus that all the world should be taxed."*

Shocked radio operators on ships and wireless owners at newspapers, who were used to Morse code heard over tiny speakers, were interrupted by a speaking voice reading Luke. They had no idea where it came from. Imagine their surprise.

When the professor finished his reading, he picked up his violin and played "O Holy Night".. the first song ever played over the air waves in the whole world.

"Oh, Holy Night" a very popular hymn today, was written by an atheist, composed by a Jew, and banned by the church leaders of the day.

Bearing Burdens for Christ
Theme: *The Loads We Carry Fulfill the Law of Christ*

21ST WEEK

INSIDE TRACK MEMORY VERSES	MIDDLE LANE SUPPORTING PASSAGES	FAST TRACK TOPICAL CHAPTERS
☐ MONDAY *Bear one another's burdens, and so fulfill the law of Christ.* Galatians 6: 2 ESV	☐ MONDAY 1 Corinthians 8:9-13 1 Corinthians 9:19-23 Proverbs 3:27-35	☐ MONDAY **Galatians 6**
☐ TUESDAY *Do not neglect to do good and to share what you have, for such sacrifices are pleasing to God.* Hebrews 13: 16 ESV	☐ TUESDAY Romans 12:9-21 Philippians 4:14-19 1 Thessalonians 4:9-12	☐ TUESDAY **Hebrews 13**
☐ WEDNESDAY *Religion that is pure and undefiled before God the Father is this: to visit orphans and widows in their affliction, and to keep oneself unstained from the world.* James 1: 27	☐ WEDNESDAY Matthew 25:31-46 Deuteronomy 14:27-29 Job 31:16-23	☐ WEDNESDAY **James 1**
☐ THURSDAY *Then the LORD said to Cain, "Where is Abel your brother?" He said, "I do not know; am I my brother's keeper?"* Genesis 4: 9 ESV	☐ THURSDAY Hebrews 12:22-29 1 Peter 1:22-25 James 4:1-6	☐ THURSDAY **Genesis 4**
☐ FRIDAY *Owe no one anything, except to love each other, for the one who loves another has fulfilled the law.* Romans 13: 8 ESV	☐ FRIDAY Matthew 7:12-23 John 13:31-35 2 Corinthians 5:14-21	☐ FRIDAY **Romans 13,14,15**

 QUESTION:
Is Self-centeredness Wrong?

ANSWER: Short answer, *"Do nothing out of selfish ambition or vain conceit. Rather, in humility value others above yourselves, not looking to your own interests but each of you to the interests of the others"* (Philippians 2:3–4 NIV).

But Jesus said, *"Love your neighbor as yourself"* (Mark 12:31). Looking out for ourselves is the first law of preservation. We learn to love others by knowing the love we have for ourselves. Thus, our love for ourselves is the model, or standard, for the love we extend to others.

The longer answer is that self-centeredness is a matter of "immoderate concern with one's own interests and well-being or self-love (egotism)" over our love for others.

Self-centeredness usurps God's commands to love and care for our neighbors (John 13:34–35), to not pass judgment on others (Romans 14:13), to bear others' burdens (Galatians 6:2), and to be kind and forgiving (Ephesians 4:32). Self-centeredness is a sin because it leads to being devoted to self-gratification and overlooking other people's needs (Romans 2:8; James 3:16).

Jesus said, *"Whoever wants to be my disciple must deny themselves and take up their cross and follow me"* (Matthew 16:24). The results of this directive for a Christian is to become centered on God, not self. Self-denial is at the core of our discipleship. The command of Christ is clear,

"No one should seek their own good, but the good of others" (1 Corinthians 10:24).

Middle Lane and Inside Track by Myra Anderson

Another Chapter from God's Book - 9th BIBLE READING MARATHON

The Last Mile of the Way

1908

By Johnson Oatman, Jr. 1856-1922

If I walk in the pathway of duty,
If I work till the close of the day,
I shall see the great King in His beauty
When I've gone the last mile of the way.

Refrain:
When I've gone the last mile of the way,
I will rest at the close of the day,
And I know there are joys that await me
When I've gone the last mile of the way.

If for Christ I proclaim the glad story,
If I seek for His sheep gone astray,
I am sure He will show me His glory
When I've gone the last mile of the way.

[Refrain]

Here the dearest of ties we must sever,
Tears of sorrow are seen ev'ry day,
But no sickness, no sighing forever
When I've gone the last mile of the way.

[Refrain]

And if here I have earnestly striven,
And have tried all His will to obey,
'Twill enhance all the rapture of heaven
When I've gone the last mile of the way.

[Refrain]

A spiritual song which looks forward to that time when each of us will have finished our course is "The Last Mile of the Way" written by Johnson Oatman Jr. (1856-1922). The son of a well-known singer, Oatman was an insurance salesman and Methodist preacher who became a prolific hymn text writer. Some of his beloved songs that have appeared in our books include "Count Your Blessings," "Hand In Hand With Jesus," "Higher Ground," "I'll Be A Friend to Jesus," "Lift Him Up," "Sweeter Than All," "No, Not One," and "What Shall It Profit?" The tune was composed by William Edie Marks.

Perhaps the theme of the song is stated in the first stanza: *"If I walk in the pathway of duty, if I work till the close of the day."* Our assurance of salvation is conditioned on *"... if we walk in the light as He is in the light, we have fellowship with one another, and the blood of Jesus His Son cleanses us from all sin"* (1 John 1:5-7).

The great joy of "The Last Mile of the Way" is in the last stanza: *"And if I have earnestly striven, And have tried all His will to obey"* then heaven will be even more wonderful.

Then, the *refrain* links our faith and our obedience to the blood of Christ. That connection, by God's grace, not only gives meaning to our lives, but saves us eternally as well! Eternal life is couched in both the joy of heaven and the rest from our strivings.

Faithful obedience becomes a loving act of grace as we learn to live in view of heaven.

Faith and Obedience
Theme: *We Must Faithfully Obey God*

22ND WEEK

INSIDE TRACK MEMORY VERSES	MIDDLE LANE SUPPORTING PASSAGES	FAST TRACK TOPICAL CHAPTERS
☐ **MONDAY** *Teach me, O LORD, the way of your statutes;* *and I will keep it to the end.* Psalm 119: 33 ESV	☐ **MONDAY** Psalm 101:1-2 Deuteronomy 4:13-14 Proverbs 11:19	☐ **MONDAY** Psalm 119
☐ **TUESDAY** *Create in me a clean heart, O God,* *and renew a right spirit within me.* Psalm 51: 10 ESV	☐ **TUESDAY** Psalm 101:3-8 Proverbs 11:20-21 Ezekiel 18:30-32	☐ **TUESDAY** Psalm 51
☐ **WEDNESDAY** *And all these blessings* *shall come upon you and overtake you,* *if you obey the voice of the LORD your God.* Deuteronomy 28: 2 ESV	☐ **WEDNESDAY** Exodus 15:23-27 Exodus 23:20-33 Leviticus 26:1-28	☐ **WEDNESDAY** Deuteronomy 28
☐ **THURSDAY** *But Peter and the apostles answered,* *We must obey God rather than men.* Acts 5: 29 ESV	☐ **THURSDAY** Acts 4:13-22 John 6:22-29 1 Peter 2:11-25	☐ **THURSDAY** Acts 5
☐ **FRIDAY** *If you love me,* *you will keep my commandments.* John 14: 15 ESV	☐ **FRIDAY** 1 John 5:1-5 2 John 1:4-11 Proverbs 2:1-15	☐ **FRIDAY** John 14

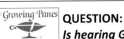 **QUESTION:**
Is hearing God's Word enough to be saved?

ANSWER: No! You must act on what you hear! That simple. James says, "Be doers of the Word and not just listeners" (James 1:22).

This rather long passage says it all: *"Not everyone who says to me, 'Lord, Lord,' will enter the kingdom of heaven, but the one who does the will of my Father who is in heaven. On that day many will say to me, 'Lord, Lord, did we not prophesy in your name, and cast out demons in your name, and do many mighty works in your name?' And then will I declare to them, 'I never knew you; depart from me, you workers of lawlessness.'*

*"Everyone then who hears these words of mine and **does them** will be like a wise man who built his house on the rock. And the* rain fell, and the floods came, and the winds blew and beat on that house, but it did not fall, because it had been founded on the rock. And everyone who hears these words of mine and **does not do them** will be like a foolish man who built his house on the sand. And the rain fell, and the floods came, and the winds blew and beat against that house, and it fell, and great was the fall of it" (Matthew 7:21-27 ESV).

The Word of God is not just a beautiful piece of literature to be enjoyed. God's Word is the perfect law of liberty: *"If you abide in my word, you are truly my disciples, and you will know the truth, and the truth will set you free"* (John 8:31–32, ESV).

It is a matter of love. Jesus said, *"If anyone loves Me, he will keep My word. My Father will love him, and We will come to him and make Our home with him. Whoever does not love Me does not keep My words"* (John 14:23).

Middle Lane and Inside Track by Homer Anderson

Another Chapter from God's Book - 9th BIBLE READING MARATHON

To God Be the Glory

1870

By Fanny Crosby 1820—1915

To God be the glory, great things he hath done:
so loved he the world that he gave us his son,
who yielded his life an atonement for sin,
and opened the life gate that all may go in.

Refrain:
Praise the Lord, praise the Lord, let the earth hear his voice!
Praise the Lord, praise the Lord, let the people rejoice!
O come to the Father, through Jesus the Son,
and give him the glory, great things he hath done.

Oh, perfect redemption, the purchase of blood,
to ev'ry believer the promise of God.
The vilest offender who truly believes,
that moment from Jesus a pardon receives.

[Refrain]

Great things he hath taught us, great things he hath done,
and great our rejoicing through Jesus the Son,
but purer, and higher, and greater will be
our wonder, our transport, when Jesus we see.

[Refrain]

This text is unique from Crosby's other hymns because, rather than focus on our experience of God, the words are wholly about God and His perfect glory. In a sense, the hymn removes us from the pedestal on which we so often place ourselves. We like to be in control and present our own image to the world, an image we are always seeking to improve.

But we are made in the image of God, and whatever we do must bring Him and Him alone the glory.

Our lives are wrapped up in God, and so too are the mistakes we make, the wounds we inflict, and all of our shortcomings. These are the things we try to avoid while we maintain control of our lives.

But what a joy and a comfort to know that God is still glorified because God is ultimately in control.

While we should still try to live a holy and upright life, we should do so to bring God glory, not ourselves. What a beautiful freedom that is!

The last line, written by a woman blind from birth, speaks of the "purer, higher, and greater wonder when we *see* Jesus!

Wisdom

Theme: *The Wisdom of God and the Wisdom of Men*

23RD WEEK

INSIDE TRACK MEMORY VERSES	MIDDLE LANE SUPPORTING PASSAGES	FAST TRACK TOPICAL CHAPTERS
MONDAY *The law of the LORD is perfect, refreshing the soul.* *The statutes of the LORD are trustworthy,* *making wise the simple.* Psalm 19:7 NIV	**MONDAY** Job 28:12-28 Proverb 1:5-33 Proverbs 2:1-20	**MONDAY** **1 Kings 3, 4**
TUESDAY *A wise heart will receive commandments,* *but foolish lips will come to ruin.* Proverbs 10:8 BSB	**TUESDAY** Proverbs 13:20 Matthew 11:16-19 James 3:13-18	**TUESDAY** **Proverbs 3, 8**
WEDNESDAY *It is because of him that you are in Christ Jesus,* *who has become for us wisdom from God--that is,* *our righteousness, holiness and redemption.* 1 Corinthians 1:30 NIV	**WEDNESDAY** Jeremiah 23:5 Matthew 7:24-29 1 Corinthians 2:6-16	**WEDNESDAY** **1 Corinthians 1**
THURSDAY *For the wisdom of this world is folly with God.* *for it is written,* *He catches the wise in their craftiness.* 1 Corinthians 3:19 ESV	**THURSDAY** Proverbs 9:1-12 Ecclesiastes 9:13-18 2 Timothy 3:12-17	**THURSDAY** **Ecclesiastes 7**
FRIDAY *If any of you lacks wisdom, let him ask God,* *who gives generously to all without reproach,* *and it will be given him.* James 1:5 ESV	**FRIDAY** Mark 12:28-34 1 Timothy 4:1-6 Titus 3:9-10	**FRIDAY** **Colossians 2**

 **QUESTION:**

What is Godly Wisdom?

ANSWER: The best answer to this question is to first review a general definition of wisdom. Wisdom is knowing how to act on knowledge in any current situation.

Wisdom sees the big picture, in focus, each part in its proper relationship. You can have knowledge without wisdom, but you cannot have wisdom without knowledge. Wisdom is the ability to integrate your knowledge and your experience with the values and beliefs you hold.

Godly wisdom comes from God, *"But if any of you lacks wisdom, let him ask of God"* (James 1:5). From His Word! *"Let the word of Christ dwell in you richly, teaching and admonishing one another in all wisdom…"* (Colossians 3:16); and from our fellow-travelers, *"Whoever walks with the wise becomes wise, but the companion of fools will suffer harm"* (Proverbs 13:20).

Godly wisdom honors God. It starts with the fear (respect) of God and results in a dedicated life of serving Him. With godly wisdom, we trade earthly values for biblical values (1 John 2:15–16). Godly wisdom means we strive to see life from God's perspective in deciding how to live.

There are different kinds of wisdom. The Bible says, "For the wisdom of this world is foolishness in God's sight" (1 Corinthians 3:19). With worldly wisdom, we may become educated, street-smart, and have "common sense" that enables us to play the world's game successfully. Godly wisdom enables us to live well in this life and to prepare ourselves for eternity.

One with Godly wisdom stands on the twin peaks of time and spiritual maturity through experience to make godly decisions for both today and the future.

Count Your Blessings

1897

By Johnson Oatman, Jr.

When upon life's billows you are tempest tossed,
When you are discouraged, thinking all is lost,
Count your many blessings, name them one by one,
And it will surprise you what the Lord hath done.

Refrain:
Count your blessings, name them one by one;
Count your blessings, see what God hath done;
Count your blessings, name them one by one;
Count your many blessings, see what God hath done.

Are you ever burdened with a load of care?
Does the cross seem heavy you are called to bear?
Count your many blessings, ev'ry doubt will fly,
And you will be singing as the days go by.

[Refrain]

When you look at others with their lands and gold,
Think that Christ has promised you His wealth untold;
Count your many blessings, money cannot buy
Your reward in heaven, nor your home on high.

[Refrain]

So, amid the conflict, whether great or small,
Do not be discouraged, God is over all;
Count your many blessings, angels will attend,
Help and comfort give you to your journey's end.

[Refrain]

Johnson Oatman wrote the text for *"When Upon Life's Billows you are Tempest Tossed"* in 1897. Growing up, Oatman realized that he would never be a great singer or preacher, but he eventually discovered his passion: hymn writing.

He became a prolific writer and wrote over 5000 hymns throughout his lifetime. Most hymnals published today have at least one of his songs. Instead of being discouraged by his lack of musical oratory skills, Oatman found hope in his ability to write.

One reason this song has been so universally included in hymnals may be because it reminds discouraged Christians of God's love and grace. We are so blessed!

It is often easy to take a negative view of life, but when we remember the things we have been given, we cannot deny that we are blessed.

The hymn proclaims that all power belongs to God, and that he desires to bless us. The lyrics for this hymn are related to several scripture passages:

"Blessed is the man who has made the LORD his trust, who has not turned to the proud, nor to those who lapse into falsehood. Many, O LORD my God, are the wonders You have done, and the plans You have for us— none can compare to You— if I proclaim and declare them, they are more than I can count."-Psalm 40:6-7

See also Psalm 107:31; Ephesians 1:3; and 1 Thessalonians 5:18.

Growing Panes

Blessings

24TH WEEK

Theme: *Count Your Blessings, Name Them One by One*

INSIDE TRACK *MEMORY VERSES*	MIDDLE LANE *SUPPORTING PASSAGES*	FAST TRACK *TOPICAL CHAPTERS*
☐ MONDAY *Jesus said to him,* *"Have you believed because you have seen me? Blessed are* *those who have not seen and yet have believed."* John 20:29 ESV	☐ MONDAY **Exodus 34: 5-7** **Proverbs 28: 13** **Romans 2: 9-11**	☐ MONDAY Psalm 32
☐ TUESDAY *Blessed is the man* *who walks not in the counsel of the wicked,* *nor stands in the way of sinners, nor sits in the seat of scoffers;* Psalm 1:1 ESV	☐ TUESDAY **Proverbs 19:17** **John 7: 37-38** **Hebrews 6:10**	☐ TUESDAY Matthew 5, 6,7
☐ WEDNESDAY *And all these blessings* *shall come upon you and overtake you,* *if you obey the voice of the LORD your God.* Deuteronomy 28:2 ESV	☐ WEDNESDAY **Deuteronomy 28: 1-6** **Psalm 34: 15-18** **I Corinthians 10:13**	☐ WEDNESDAY Job 5
☐ THURSDAY *A faithful man will abound with blessings,* *but whoever hastens to be rich* *will not go unpunished.* Proverbs 28:20 ESV	☐ THURSDAY **Psalms 70: 1-5** **Hebrew 10: 5-7** **I Peter 5:7**	☐ THURSDAY Psalm 40
☐ FRIDAY *Blessed be the God and Father of our Lord Jesus Christ,* *who has blessed us in Christ with every* *spiritual blessing in the heavenly places* Ephesians 1:3 ESV	☐ FRIDAY **Psalms 25: 15** **Psalm 140: 4,5** **Proverbs 23: 1-8**	☐ FRIDAY Psalm 141

Growing Pains

QUESTION:
What are Spiritual Blessings?

ANSWER: Being *blessed* comes from the Greek term *makarios*, which means "fortunate," "happy," "enlarged," or "lengthy." The word is used in the Scriptures to define the kind of happiness that comes from receiving favor from God. *Blessed* can also be translated "favored" concerning Mary being chosen to be the mother of Jesus (Luke 1).

Spiritual blessings are much more significant than material blessings such as food, shelter, or good fortune.

The Beatitudes (Matthew 5:3-12) describe the inner quality of a faithful servant of God. This blessedness is <u>a spiritual state of well-being</u> and prosperity—a deep, joy-filled contentment that cannot be shaken by poverty, grief, famine, persecution, war, or any other trial or tragedy we face in life.

Those spiritually blessed <u>trust in God's love</u>: "Can anything ever separate us from Christ's love? Does it mean he no longer loves us if we have trouble or calamity, or are persecuted, or hungry, or destitute, or in danger, or threatened with death? . . . No, despite all these things, overwhelming victory is ours through Christ, who loved us. And I am convinced that nothing can ever separate us from God's love. Neither death nor life, neither angels nor demons, neither our fears for today nor our worries about tomorrow—not even the powers of hell can separate us from God's love. No power in the sky above or in the earth below—indeed, nothing in all creation will ever be able to separate us from the love of God that is revealed in Christ Jesus our Lord" (Romans 8:35–39, NLT).

All...**ALL**(!!!) spiritual blessings are IN CHRIST! We are so **favored** to be in the spiritual body of Christ to experience the full impact of God in our lives now and for all eternity. So blessed!

Middle Lane and Inside Track by Janet Brown

Another Chapter from God's Book - 9th BIBLE READING MARATHON

I Love to Tell the Story

1866

1869 Refrain

By Kate Hankey and William G. Fischer

I love to tell the story of unseen things above:
of Jesus and his glory, of Jesus and his love.
I love to tell the story, because I know 'tis true.
It satisfies my longings as nothing else could do.

Refrain:
I love to tell the story,
'twill be my theme in glory,
to tell the old, old story
of Jesus and his love.

I love to tell the story. 'Tis pleasant to repeat
what seems, each time I tell it, more wonderfully sweet.
I love to tell the story, for some have never heard
the message of salvation from God's own holy word.

[Refrain]

I love to tell the story, for those who know it best
seem hungering and thirsting to hear it, like the rest.
And when, in scenes of glory, I sing the new, new song,
'twill be the old, old story that I have loved so long.

[Refrain]

Katherine Hankey is the author of this text. While recovering from a serious illness in 1866, she wrote a very long poem about the story of Christ in multiple parts, which was published in different versions. The text of this hymn was most likely taken from the second part of the poem called "The Story Told," even though the hymn does not tell the story at all, but refers to the great joy the story has given to disciples of Jesus.

This is a story of the great love God has for us. The themes of this text are the personal value of the story of redemption to a particular Christian, and the importance of telling that story to others. It is a story of evangelism to tell the world of God's love.

In "The Story Told," which is part two of the poem "The Old, Old Story" from which this hymn is taken, Katherine Hankey briefly summarizes the whole story of the Bible, from the Fall in Genesis 3 to Christ's birth, death, and resurrection to the "scenes of glory" in Revelation. This hymn is a good reminder that the story of God and His people throughout the ages should be a focus of Christians. When we speak to others of the gospel, we must tell them "the old, old story of Jesus and His love."

Love

25TH WEEK

Theme: *Now, The Greatest of These is Love*

INSIDE TRACK — MEMORY VERSES	MIDDLE LANE — SUPPORTING PASSAGES	FAST TRACK — TOPICAL CHAPTERS
MONDAY *He that loveth not knoweth not God; for God is love.* 1 John 4:8 KJV	**MONDAY** 1 John 2: 15-17 1 John 3: 10-16 1 John 4: 7-11	**MONDAY** 1 John 1, 2, 3, 4
TUESDAY *This is love, that we walk according to His commandments. This is the commandment, that as you have heard from the beginning, you should walk in it.* 2 John 1: 6 NKJV	**TUESDAY** 2 John 1: 4-6 Romans 12: 9-13 Luke 10: 25-28	**TUESDAY** 2 John 1
WEDNESDAY *You shall love the LORD your God with all your heart and with all your soul and with all your might.* Deuteronomy 6:5 ESV	**WEDNESDAY** Hosea 3: 1-5 Matthew 5: 43-46 Joshua 22: 4-6	**WEDNESDAY** Hosea 3
THURSDAY *This is My commandment, that you love one another, just as I have loved you.* John 15:12 NASB	**THURSDAY** Psalm 31: 23-24 Psalm 145: 17-21 1 Corinthians 13: 4-7	**THURSDAY** Psalm 136
FRIDAY *So now faith, hope, and love abide, these three; but the greatest of these is love.* 1 Corinthians 13: 13 ESV	**FRIDAY** 1 Corinthians 13: 1-3 1 Corinthians 13: 5-10 Matthew 22: 34-40	**FRIDAY** 1 Corinthians 13

QUESTION: *What Can Separate us from God's Love?*

ANSWER: Short answer, *NOTHING!*

Why not? Because *"God showed his great love for us by sending Christ to die for us while we were still sinners"* (Romans 5:8). The death of His only son for our sins shows the powerful love of God for us.

Perhaps the greatest verses in the greatest chapter of the Bible are found in Romans 8:31-39: *"...If God is for us, who can ever be against us? Since he did not spare even his own Son but gave him up for us all, won't he also give us everything else?... Can anything ever separate us from Christ's love? Does it mean he no longer loves us if we have trouble or calamity, or are persecuted, or hungry, or destitute, or in danger, or threatened with death?... No, despite all these things, overwhelming victory is ours through Christ, who loved us.*

And I am convinced that nothing can ever separate us from God's love. Neither death nor life, neither angels nor demons, neither our fears for today nor our worries about tomorrow—not even the powers of hell can separate us from God's love. No power in the sky above or in the earth below—indeed, nothing in all creation will ever be able to separate us from the love of God that is revealed in Christ Jesus our Lord."

God does not promise us a life free of affliction, but He will be with us through anything we face. God's love is in constant supply for believers in Jesus Christ (Romans 5:5). We can count on His love in the normal calamities of life and be fully assured of it in the crisis of death. When we feel unloved, the problem is our love, not God's love.

Middle Lane and Inside Track by John Hunt

Amazing Grace

1779

By John Newton 1725—1807

Amazing grace! how sweet the sound,
that saved a wretch like me!
I once was lost, but now am found;
was blind, but now I see.

'Twas grace that taught my heart to fear,
and grace my fears relieved.
How precious did that grace appear
the hour I first believed.

Through many dangers, toils, and snares
I have already come.
'Tis grace has brought me safe thus far,
and grace will lead me home.

When we've been there ten thousand years,
bright shining as the sun,
we've no less days to sing God's praise
than when we'd first begun.

If America had a national folk hymn, this would probably be it. This well-loved and oft-sung hymn, written by John Newton in the late eighteenth century, is a powerful assurance and declaration of the grace of God working in all our lives.

Newton lived a pretty tough life in his earlier days while at sea in the Navy, eventually becoming captain of a slave ship. Newton later wrote, *"I can see no reason why the Lord singled me out for mercy…unless it was to show, by one astonishing instance, that with him, nothing is impossible!"*

As we sing the very familiar words of this hymn, how powerful it is to think of ourselves as an "astonishing instance" of God's grace and mercy.

The original text has not been altered very much, though some additions have been made – Chris Tomlin's added refrain, for example: *"My chains are gone, I've been set free - my God my Savior has ransomed me. And like a flood, his mercy reigns; unending love, amazing grace."*

26TH WEEK

The End In Sight

Theme: *"Yes, I Am Coming Soon. Amen. Come, Lord Jesus"*

INSIDE TRACK MEMORY VERSES	MIDDLE LANE SUPPORTING PASSAGES	FAST TRACK TOPICAL CHAPTERS
☐ MONDAY - *I am the good shepherd. The good shepherd lays down His life for the sheep.* John 10: 11 BSB	☐ MONDAY Ezekiel 34: 1-31 Matthew 25: 31-32	☐ MONDAY Psalm 23
☐ TUESDAY - *Let us hear the conclusion of the whole matter: Fear God, and keep his commandments: for this is the whole duty of man.* Ecclesiastes 12:13-14 KJV	☐ TUESDAY Job 28: 27-28 1 John 3: 21-24 Romans 8: 15-39	☐ TUESDAY Ecclesiastes 12
☐ WEDNESDAY *And as it is appointed unto men once to die, but after this the judgment.* Hebrews 9: 27 KJV	☐ WEDNESDAY Psalm 89: 46-52 Hebrews 11: 4-6 Genesis 5: 18-24	☐ WEDNESDAY 2 Kings 2
☐ THURSDAY - *It teaches us to say "No" to ungodliness and worldly passions, and to live self-controlled, upright and godly lives in this present age.* Titus 2: 1 BSB	☐ THURSDAY Philippians 3: 19-21 Colossians 1: 3-14 Ephesians 4: 17-32	☐ THURSDAY Acts 1
☐ FRIDAY *Behold, I am coming soon, and My reward is with Me, to give to each one according to what he has done. I am the Alpha and the Omega, the First and the Last, the Beginning and the End.* Revelation 22: 12 BSB	☐ FRIDAY Revelation 6: 1-2 John 5: 19-30 2 Peter 3: 8-18	☐ FRIDAY Revelation 19, 20,21, & 22

Growing Panes

QUESTION:
Are You Prepared for the End?

ANSWER: This question is about the end of life, or the end of all things in the last days and whether we will be saved or lost eternally. We do not know when either of these two events will come. The Bible says we do not know even what will happen tomorrow (James 4:14), or the next hour!

What is important is being prepared for either event (Matthew 25:1-13). So, this week's question may be answered best with other questions.

Are you spiritually a child of God? If so, you have been "born again" (John 3:1-21). You have gone from the kingdom of darkness into the kingdom of light (Colossians 1:13). You have been delivered by your faith and obedience when your sins were washed away in the act of baptism (Acts 22:16; Acts 8:36-39; 1 Peter 3:21).

Are you a new person in Christ? A new person is holy and righteous in living for Christ (Ephesians 4:17-32). If you are a new person, you put off the old man of sin. You walk in the light (1 John 1:6-7).

Do you put the Kingdom of God first in your life? How you answer this question is perhaps the most telling! What is the most important thing in life for you? Jesus said, "Seek the Kingdom of God" above all else (Matthew 6:33 NLT).

More important,

Do you trust God and are you faithful to obey him!? Jesus is the *one way* to enter the portals of heaven (John 14:6). Like the hymn says, "Trust and obey! For there is no other way!" So, you answer the question. Yes, or No!

All Tracks by G. R. Holton

- Final Review -

Write one sentence to describe ONE lesson you have learned by reading the Bible Reading Marathon for each of the weeks. ONE THOUGHT that summarizes the topic of the week. If you need to, go back and review each week, including the memory verses, to refresh your memory.

Week 1
OUR GOD: **The Majesty of Almighty God**

Week 2
GLORY OF GOD: **The Incomparable Glory of Our God**

Week 3
GOD'S WORLD: **The Created, Spiritual and Worldly Universe**

Week 4
CONDEMNED BY SIN: **God Gave the World Up to Sin**

Week 5
TRUE WORSHIP: **Acceptable Worship in Spirit and Truth**

Week 6
VAIN & FALSE WORSHIP: **Unacceptable Worship and Idol Worship**

Week 7
PRAISE AND PRAYER: **Bless the Lord, O My soul**

Week 8
GIVING TO GOD: **Opening the Windows of Heaven**

Week 9
GOD'S FAITHFULNESS: **Be Faithful**

Week 10
LEADERS FOR CHRIST: **Do as I have done, Pick up your Towel**

Week 11
UNBELIEF AND DISOBEDIENCE: **Ungodliness and disobedience**

Week 12
RIGHTEOUSNESS: **Things that Pertain to Life and Godliness**

Week 13
NEW BEGINNINGS: **Again! Starting Over.**

Week 14
SEEKING THE LOST: **Come Unto Me, I will Give You Rest**

Week 15
VICTORY IN JESUS: **The Greatness of God's Powers**

Week 16
GOD PROVIDES: **Search Me, O God, and Know My Heart**

Week 17
GOD'S PROTECTION: **Be Strong in the Power of His Might**

Week 18
MARRIAGE: **God Joins a Man and a Woman in Marriage**

Week 19
FREEDOM IN SERVING GOD: **In Matters of Faith and Opinions**

Week 20
SPIRITUAL FOOD: **Food that Satisfies Our Spiritual Desires**

Week 21
BEARING BURDENS: **Loads we Carry Fulfil the Law of Christ**

Week 22
FAITH AND OBEDIENCE: **We Must Faithfully Obey God**

Week 23
WISDOM: **The Wisdom of God and the Wisdom of Men**

Week 24
BLESSINGS: **Count Your Blessings, Name Them One by One**

Week 25
LOVE: **The Greatest of These is Love**

Week 26
THE END IN SIGHT: **Come Lord Jesus**

Congratulations!

You have completed your 26-week BRM spiritual training program! GREAT!

⇒ *You have more spiritual stamina to face the challenges of daily living*

⇒ *You have gained in the ability to "run the race" of Christian living with endurance*

⇒ *Your spiritual health is improved!*

"…you will be a worthy servant of Christ Jesus, one who is nourished by the message of faith and the good teaching you have followed. Do not waste time arguing over godless ideas and old wives' tales. Instead, train yourself to be godly. Physical training is good, but training for godliness is much better, promising benefits in this life and in the life to come" - 1 Timothy 4: 6-8b NLT